The
Adlerian Team Leader

Or Berkovitch

To Danielle and Roni,
My beloved daughters
And greatest teachers.

Contents

ACKNOWLEDGMENTS

"The Adlerian Team Leader" uses a psychological theory applied to educating modern children and adapts it as a management theory for use in the software industry.

I was first formally introduced to the Adlerian theory by Mrs. Ruth Dafni-Harel whom I'd like to thank for her teaching and guidance.

To my parents, I'd like to thank for the natural "Adlerian" way in which my brother, my sister and I were raised. My parent's education filled with positive experiences, a great deal of encouragement, tolerance and everything they could do to enhance our lives. My children and spouse benefit from that inherited approach – and now, my employees and colleagues as well.

I'd also like to thank Mrs. Bella Paz, for her guidance in the field of education and for contributing her knowledge, wisdom, and experience to anyone willing to listen.

And finally, I would like to thank my darling wife, who stands with me on everything that I do throughout our beautiful mutual journey.

Introduction

What is a Software Team Leader?

Every software development project is created by one or more teams led by a Team Leader. Who should be hired for the Team Leader position? What skills does the ideal candidate need to enable the team and the project to thrive?

Leading a software team is a HUGE challenge because the job literally clashes two very different human intelligences: the emotional quotient and the Intellectual-analytical quotient.

A Software Team Leader is a juxtaposition of responsibilities. He or she is a leader of spirit, while equally a leader of practice. These two very different skill sets need to be put into play in order to do this job successfully.

A Leader of Practice

A Team Leader solves the day-to-day issues of development; he or she needs to schedule tasks, break down complex thorny problems and much more. In most cases, the software team leader is a former developer.

There are several responsibilities and several decisions that a non-developer simply cannot fulfill: Code reviewing, refactoring, deciding on coding alternatives, choosing implementation architectures, unit testing, understanding the implications and true meaning of 'quick-and-dirty' vs. 'tidy architecture', and even some basic collegial empathy. These are part of the team leader's job - and cannot be achieved by managing tasks with a Gantt. Many software projects fail because of the details - and code projects are all about the little details. Professional team leaders must be able to manage tasks and people, but they also must be able to delve into the code and make the best possible decisions there.

When a non-former developer is appointed to the job of "team leader", he or she usually does the job of project manager, a product manager or something of that ilk. A non-developer will lack critical skills required to perform the tasks of a team leader.

A Leader of Spirit

However, the jump from managing lines of code to managing real human beings is sharp. A good team leader needs to know how to lead the people to success, in addition to solving the technical problems.

As it turns out, the set of skills required to be a great developer are not the same set of skills required to lead a development team, And as developers are the team leaders, teaching leadership to developers thrust into leadership is critical.

How does a developer usually get promoted to team leader? What are the criteria? Was he or she recognized as an excellent developer? Did he/she create an extraordinary piece of code that helped progress a project? Was the promotion based on team seniority? Some are promoted to team leader because of their innate approach to leadership, however even in these cases, these exceptionally talented people often have not had access to relevant and critical leadership training.

Peter Principle

Becoming a team leader is usually akin to the "Peter Principle". While the principle is often cited in the mocking "people rise to the level of their own incompetence", the more serious application is actually a crucial point: The Peter Principle is a management theory that states that people are usually considered for promotion based on their performance in their present position, with the skill sets that position requires and not for projected performance in their future role. Team leaders, therefore, are often selected not for their leadership skills, but for their awesomeness as developers.

Yet, if you are a great developer, and dream about developing the next-generation-what-ever, then becoming a team leader is the wrong step towards that goal. The world needs ninja-developers. Your company needs hands-on leaders. A ninja-developer becoming a team leader might actually harm your company and not help it at all.

You should, however, become a team leader if you love code, know how to problem solve, but most importantly, are willing to learn the skills necessary to lead others towards success.

Becoming a Team Leader

So - you are a developer, and you are excited about the prospect of leading the team. How do you approach this daunting task? How do you organize around this new responsibility? First - you need to focus on your team. Ask yourself: who are they and what do they want? You may think this is self-evident, as you were just a member of said team - but now you are looking at it from a different perspective. How will you get them to achieve their goals?

Your Position in the Organization

What is the team leader's position in the organization? This is not written in stone, but something that you will determine for yourself. **One thing is for sure, though - you are NOT the "autistic" ninja developer that you were just a while ago.** You're now playing in a much different field - the organizational field. You're a focal point of business goals. You're a focal point of recruitment and of training. You generate the information required to take decisions that affect your company.

Team leaders have many interfaces and a constant goal of serving and communicating with these interfaces in order to get the job done. As a team leader - you have to decide your approach towards each of the interfaces. Do you plan to compete with your colleague team leaders? What will you do when the product manager asks you for a "favor" that is beyond the scope of your daily commitments to your development manager? Do you actively look for promotion in other development managers' offices, or will you rely on your development manager to eventually help you grow in the organization?

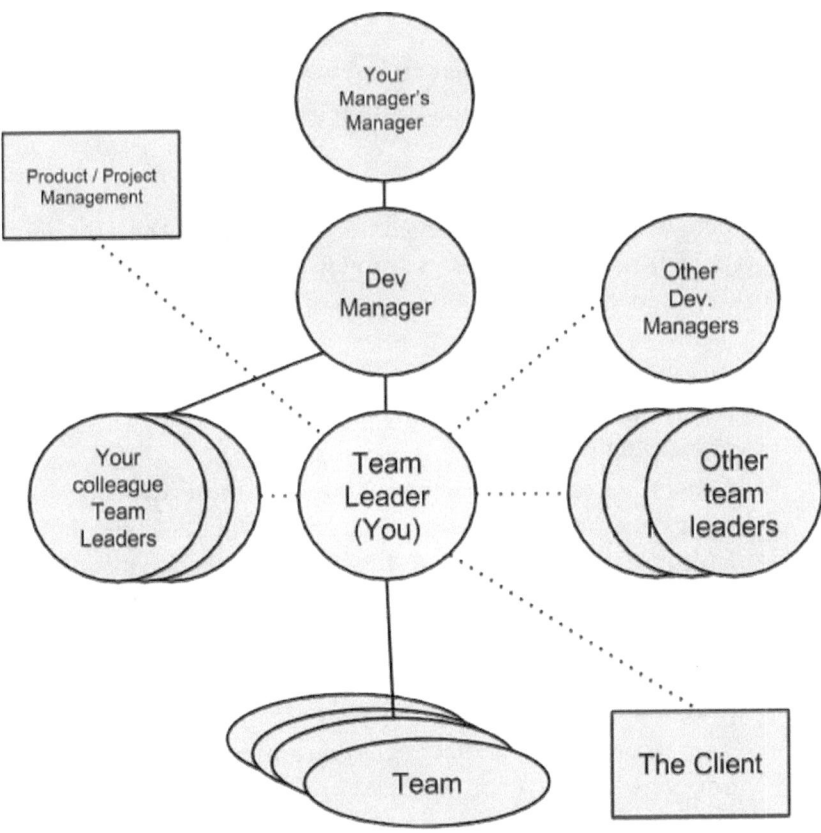

Understand a Developer's Soul

So, as a development team leader, take a step back and think about your developers.

What motivates them? What makes them passionate about what they do? You must understand their internal motivation in order to lead them to success. The best description I ever read on a developer's internal motivation was in the milestone book "The Mythical Man Month" by Frederick P. Brooks, Jr. Brooks describes the joys and woes of the craft:

The craft of programming "gratifies creative longings built deep within us and delights sensibilities we have in common with all men," providing five kinds of joys:

- The joy of making things.
- The joy of making things that are useful to other people.
- The fascination of fashioning puzzle-like objects of interlocking moving parts.
- The joy of always learning, of a non-repeating task.
- The delight of working in a medium so tractable, pure thought-stuff which nevertheless exists, moves, and works in a way that world-objects do not.

Likewise the craft has special woes inherent in it.

- Adjusting to the requirement of perfection is the hardest part of learning to program.
- Others set one's objectives and one must depend upon things (especially programs) one cannot control; the authority is not equal to the responsibility. This sounds worse than it is: actual authority comes from momentum of accomplishment.
- With any creativity come dreary hours of painstaking labor; programming is no exception.
- The programming project converges more slowly the nearer one gets to the end, whereas one expects it to converge faster as one approaches the end.
- One's product is always threatened with obsolescence before completion. The real tiger is never a match for the paper one, unless real use is wanted.

Source: The Mythical Man-Month, Anniversary Edition, ADDISON-WESLEY, Page 231

Read this paragraph and read it again. See how it applies to your team. Are there additional motivators you would like to add to the list? Your first step is to genuinely understand what gets your team out of bed in the morning. Once you know this - you have a potent tool in helping them to succeed in their goals. Remember that your team is more than just an amorphous group, with each member responding to the same impetus. Each member of your team may have different motivators. Look for this. Respecting your employees, accepting their difference in character and point of view are vital for your team's success.

Leader vs. Manager

As a team leader, you are more than just a manager; a team leader is a leader. Search google for the long definition of the difference between the two, but in a nutshell, a manager uses his authority to achieve the team's goals while a leader uses his charisma and inspiration. Because of the nature of the job, leadership should be the primary approach of the development team leader. The nature of development is that it is a practice of detail and complexity. Every line of code might have influences far beyond the scope of a local task. A developer can't just 'take an order' and commit it. A developer has to be highly motivated to holistically groom the software system he or she is developing. The developer must be led to care for the system and for its users. Only a leader can help achieve this genuine motivation in the hearts of his staff.

As a leader, you wear a lot of hats: you set a personal example; you stay long hours when things are intense; you take responsibility for errors; you are professional about the technical material with which your team deals; you know the business side; you report to your superiors accurately and efficiently.

As a leader, you are loyal to your company. This is truly important because your loyalty empowers team members to feel that they belong to something good and important, which will encourage their tribal instincts to stick to each other and to you. A team that is devoted to each other and believes in its leader has a great deal more power and ability to succeed. But, you say - what if the loyalty is fake? What if you don't like something the company does or something about the company? Companies can be good in some things but bad in others. As a leader you need to latch on to the things that you believe in and create that loyalty within you. Pay attention to the things you like about the company and give this more space and attention. You are a leader now. You determine the team spirit.

You also are choosing to represent the company so for you to succeed, you need to believe in the place you are working. Take the time to remind yourself why you are here. Find the reasons and remind yourself. Then remind your team.

As a leader you set the standards. You lead your team towards delivering quality software. While "quality" may mean something different in each company - you are responsible to set the standards in your team to match corporate requirements. All too commonly, a new team leader joins an existing team and allows the existing team members to determine the quality according to 'what they know so far'. If this new team leader is you, you stand at a crossroad because standards are a matter of decision. You can decide whether you want to change things or conform to current standards. Beware of making too many assumptions at the beginning of your regime. Some of your team's practices were written in sweat and tears. Investigate your people's point of view with deep, profound questions. Why are they doing what they are doing? Why do they follow a certain practice? What led to a certain approach? You will often find that many of the things are the way they are as a result of emotional decisions rather than professional.

The Team Leader Dilemma

Because of your background as a developer, and in light of your new managerial responsibilities - you will be torn between two paths in pursuing your goals: Develop or Manage. This is "The Team Leader Dilemma". The Team Leader Dilemma is a central principle you should take with you after reading this book. It is an important prism through which to look at the actions you will be taking every single day.

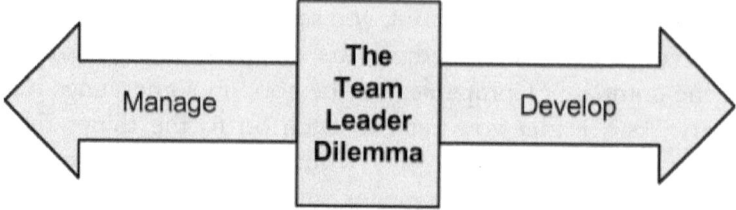

Develop

There are times when you will just HAVE to delve into the details of the implementation. When a developer is stuck, when a technical problem is too hard to solve, when developers get carried away by their coding and are not completing the tasks at hand on time, you will be required to work with them on the nitty gritty details and develop. However, these are dangerous times for you as a manager. Why dangerous? Because when you delve into the details, you lose focus from your other team members. The longer you delve into the task - the greater the loss of focus.

Manage

When speaking of education administration, the saying goes: "a school is only as good as its teachers". One would imagine the development team might be "as good as its developers". In real life that is not actually the case, because in fact, the team leader is a game changer. Beyond the assumed personal coding abilities, a team leader sees the overall outlook of things. This is a strong point of view that enables the team leader to navigate the progress while jumping in to 'push' from time to time. For the majority of time - a team leader needs to manage. Not Code.

To make this all the more difficult - your manager (and life's circumstances) WILL put pressure on you when you choose either of the above. When you choose "develop" your manager will blame you for not seeing the big picture. When you choose "manage" your manager will blame you for not going into the details. This dilemma brings the most pressure to the team leader's job. This tension is real and is the main cause of the team leaders' difficulty to perform. But don't despair. There are tools to handle this inherent conflict. One thing I can assure you is that you'll never get used to it. You'll just get better at juggling between the two options.

Tools for the Team Leader Dilemma

Tools for when a team leader is in developer mode:

Developer Mode Tool #1: The quick update cycle

Take a moment out from the development task you've undertaken, and cycle through your people. You actually don't need a full discussion with your team to learn their status. Ask each team member where they are in their tasks and try NOT to comment too much on what they are doing. Remember - you didn't approach them in order to take part in their task - you're just getting an update on their situation. Deflect any discussion that goes into too much depth - because this is not the time for it. Direct them to external resources (people or information).

Developer Mode Tool #2: End Of Day Summary Email
Ask your people to report to you at the end of the day (EOD) about the results of their tasks. What have they accomplished? What difficulties have they encountered? What do they plan to do tomorrow?

Developers hate these kind of assignments, but they are actually an efficient way to control and manage the development process.

Developer Mode Tool #3: Schedule recap meetings
Should another critical task in your team occur while you are in Developer mode - schedule a recap session with the developer/s leading that task.

Developer Mode Tool #4: Deflect your manager's demand for on-site status
Your manager will want to know the status of the tasks handled by your team throughout the day. You cannot give that information on site because you are naturally not updated on other tasks at this time. Schedule an appointment with your manager for a later time. Make sure you take enough time to prepare yourself for that meeting. It can take as much as an hour(!) of preparation. That means you'll have to jump out of developer mode - run an hour in Manager mode, and later come back to Developer mode again to continue your development assignment. This is called "Managerial overhead" and it's a part of your life now.

General Note for Support of Developer Mode
Practice! Make sure you don't lose that "touch" of yours to coding. Practice at home or free up some time at work to practice your developer skills. The less rust you have to remove - the faster you'll be able to complete the development assignments imposed on you.

Tools for when a team leader is in manager mode:

Manager Mode Tool #1: Demand a plan

Ask the developer or QA for a plan about the exact steps they plan on taking to complete the task. Ask them to write down each task, with time estimates. Ask hard questions. "How are you going to do that?" Request alternatives. "Is there another way to do that?" Question if there are inevitable refactorings to do. Pay attention to the inner details of the task.

Manager Mode Tool #2: Code Review

Code review before or after a task is done. Question the implementation. Suggest alternatives. Play a bit with the code while with the developer - even if eventually you don't use the changes you're showing.

Manager Mode Tool #3: Ask for a presentation

Allot time for your developers to educate you and the rest of the team. This strengthens team spirit and also enables you to delve into the details more comfortably.

Manager Mode Tool #4: Schedule regular sessions with your developers

To make sure you're "on top of the game" - schedule development sessions with your developers (a.k.a Pair Programming). Let them guide you in their way of thought and spirit of coding. Share your knowledge with them - and your consideration.

Manager Mode Tool #5: In your free time - learn the code

Learn the code when in Manager mode. This will assist you in "going in deep" faster and more efficiently. Don't wait for things to get hot. Prepare to quickly delve into any part of your system.

Part I

The Adlerian Team Leader

Leading Your Team

Leadership comes in many forms. Previously, I introduced the issue of leadership with two ideas. First of all - acknowledge the difference between a leader and a manager. And secondly: a team leader functions from the principle of leadership.

But what is the actual definition and role of a leader? Now that you are taking on this position, it is important to look at the notion of leadership more deeply and with a critical eye.

For example: through which parameters can a leader be identified? How will you know if you are one? Is being a leader simply a matter of giving a personal example to others? Is leadership conveyed through planning ahead and "showing the way"?

Take the time to ask yourself what kind of leader you want to be. It is important to look intently at the purpose of your actions and decisions and ask yourself how your actions affect team goals.

There is no "one best way" to be a team leader. This book introduces "Adlerian Leadership", a system I found effective in building a productive, self-motivated and happy team. This simple set of tools, with a humanitarian approach at its heart, fuels the development team and drives it to success.

So, to introduce this method, I'd like to tell you a bit about the ideas behind it.

Good Leadership Reflects Society

For around 150 years following the industrial revolution - children's education was autocratic. They were taught to be disciplined and obey orders. They were raised to be "good employees" who work in production lines and manufacture efficiently. However, in our decade - this has all changed. Employees are required to be creative. Personal development is a crucial part of an employee agenda. Turnover rate in the software industry is around 1-2 years per job, a symptom of the individual's desire to grow fast and improve personal position.

To successfully engage employees, management style should ideally support their agendas and needs. Approaching management as a mandate that allows you to "boss" your employees and tell them what to do is anachronistic - and will ultimately backfire. While this may have worked in the industrial age and reflected the times, employees don't have to obey orders accurately and efficiently any more. They can get another job. It will serve you much better to understand this and tailor your approach accordingly.

Not surprisingly, modern theories of parenthood have developed frameworks and tools to deal with modern children. When I became a parent, my wife enrolled us in parenting lessons at the Adler Institute where I was first introduced to these theories by Ms. Ruth Dafni-Harel. Somewhere in the middle of the 12-lesson course I discovered that I was suddenly using parenting tools at work with my employees. It was a surprising insight to discover that in fact parenting and management have broad common ground. They both involve providing frameworks for shepherding individuals to be the best they can be.

Of course, employees are not children and I in no way intend for you to treat them as such. However, an adult's emotional structure is drawn straight from his or her childhood - and we are all in fact children of this world. Children and adults, for example, react similarly to constructive encouragement and focusing on encouragement is effective in building desired behaviors. This is a central tenet in Adlerian philosophy. So, Just like a mother or a father leading a family - a manager should lead the team and provide support for the employee's emotional needs.

Adler's Theory

Adler believed that we all have three basic desires and goals:

> To belong
> To feel significant
> To feel capable

Alfred Adler's theory claims that "when we feel encouraged, we feel capable and appreciated and will generally act in a connected and cooperative way. When we are discouraged, we may act in unhealthy ways by competing, withdrawing, or giving up".

Equality of value and mutual respect are two pillars of the Adlerian theory. We have different roles in our family cell, but we are all of equal value and deserving of respect. If a parent yells at his children or rudely criticizes them - he or she is breaching this mutual respect and equality of value. Children are not of less value than adults because they are children. Accordingly if a child is disrespectful to his parents or thinks that he can do anything that comes to mind - he, too, is breaking the rules and needs to have more defined boundaries set in place. Equality of value is a perception of life. Adler believed that we all deserve to be honored, empathized, loved, and listened to. There are a lot of people who think in "vertical" terms considering a wealthier or higher ranked person to be a better human being. Adler rejects this approach and asks that we raise our children as the unique and blessed individuals that they are, without ranking one above the other for any reason.

As with children, so with your team

You and your team members are of equal value and you must demand mutual respect between everyone on the team. Every individual is unique.
If an employee is encouraged and feels capable and appreciated - he will generally act in a connected and cooperative way. If we discourage or criticize an employee he may act in unhealthy ways by competing with his colleagues or delaying his assignments. Eventually the employee will either leave or do harm to the team and the company.

Your employees need to feel they belong to the team, that each is special in his or her own way. They must be able to contribute and feel significant. They need to feel capable of taking the team's goals and completing them with quality and on time.

There is evidence that in fact Agile theories, the industry-accepted methodologies for software development, are in essence based on the same tenets as Adlerian theory. In Scrum methodology, for example, there is a popular belief that the "Scrum Master" (team leader) shouldn't have ANY managerial authority over team members (e.g. Scrum Master != Functional Manager). The reason for this is that if a Scrum Master is required to "pull rank" on every decision - he will not lead the team but manage them with inequality. If you find yourself saying to your developers: "You are the employee and you need to do what I tell you" - you're doing things in a non-Adlerian manner. Scrum didn't want to rely on the team leader's ability to practice equality-of-value, so they removed their managerial authority and turned the team leader's job into a "Scrum Master". There's really no need for that. A Scrum Master can be a functional manager as well, only he or she must be equipped with tools to handle their teammates' emotional needs.

Use of Agile methodologies require that every team member exhibit a great deal of motivation. We are obligated to write extensive tests and to commit to iteration goals. We are obligated to collaborate with other team member and peers. We are obligated to good refactoring work and excellent implementation. So, there is hidden assumption of uniform self-motivation which, from my experience, is simply not true. Employees need to be driven and constantly motivated. The assumption of self-motivation might cause unsuccessful implementations of Agile methodologies. For example, a team leader from HP described to me in detail her team's use of Scrum. When I asked her "Do team members pull tasks from the backlog by themselves or do you assign tasks?" She responded that she hadn't yet figured out how to make them pull tasks on their own. Her assumption that Scrum would include methodology for motivation led to her troubles with the implementation of the system. Scrum doesn't include methodology to groom motivation - Scrum only grooms tasks!

"Belonging" according to Adler is a fundamental human need. It applies to ANYONE from youth to elderly. For example, when an employee arrives at a new job he or she will feel that it is most important to "find his or her place" in the new environment. They will seek the environment where they feel protected, loved, unique, and valued. Once an employee accomplishes the sense of belonging -

his or her mind is clear to handle the job itself. This is the key - clarity of thought. This is a universal concern. If a person is in a room with others and constantly troubled whether the others like them or not, the person will be busy finding his/her place and thinking counterproductive thoughts such as "do I need to be heard to be valued?" instead of listening, learning, internalizing and working. They will constantly be busy with themselves and their social positioning. Lack of confidence screens everything.

Managers are required to fill their employee's emotional vacancy first - and then move on to the work. The tools for accomplishing this are diverse but at its base is the Adlerian acknowledgement that we are all equal and that we all want the same things. The ways to achieve our goals are simply different from one person to another. Understanding and being aware of these basic human needs allows us to be empathic and see the desires behind the straightforward behavior.

We must also create an environment of trust. If we believe in the employees - they will believe in themselves. If we challenge them while encouraging them, they will find ways to accomplish remarkable achievements. This will spawn a circle of success, confidence, and independence that creates strong teams.

In the following sections I will detail Adlerian tools that together can be used as a methodology to lead your team. Here is a brief overview of the headlines:

- Encouragement and Criticism
- Equality of Value
- Assertiveness & Boundaries
- Over Protectiveness
- EIER
- Independence 0% → 100%
- Letting Go
- Belong, Significant, Capable
- Responsibility
- Taking the Initiative - avoid "reaction based"
- Setting Expectations

- Manager-Employee Time
- Disturbing Behaviors
- Power Struggles
- Managerial Consensus
- Listening & Empathizing
- Seniority & Competition
- Managerial Vision and Employee Development
- Tolerance as an Innovation Driver

Encouragement and Criticism

Encouragement feeds,
> Discouragement starves,
>> Criticism Poisons

Remember this phrase. Think about yourself when you are encouraged. Feels great to contribute, doesn't it? It feels great to know that you've done something that mattered to someone and that was beneficial in some way. Encouragement makes an individual feel that they are capable and significant. Acknowledgement for the contribution makes an individual feel that they belong to the group. The 3 Adlerian goals are achieved on the spot.

But don't fall into the encouragement pitfall of praise. There is a difference between encouragement and praise. Encouragement is specific to a certain act. It is detailed in a way that enforces and intensifies good behavior. It is constructive in nature. Praise, on the other hand, is completely amorphous. Let's examine some examples:

Encouragement –

"You did a good job planning the iteration. The design was very detailed and the execution was accurate, as were your time estimations"

"You really helped Jennifer. Your overlap agenda was very relevant and now she feels she has teammates she can rely on"

"You've kept good structure and design in your code. Your naming conventions are very effective and you employed efficient data structure manipulation"

"Although your code didn't work as planned, your research of the issue was very thorough. Try making a smaller sample application first, and then cast the results on the main code"

Praise –

"You are da man!!"

"no, no - you're the top developer man! awesome!! yeah!".

"You are the king baby!"

"This is the most awesome code I have ever seen in my life"

Encouragement enforces positive behavior. Good work is an achievement because it achieves a goal with positive implications. A developer develops a certain function very quickly? Tell the developer how grateful the users will be in their user experience. A big production problem was solved? Tell the involved teammates that they contributed to the team's reputation and that they saved money for the customer. One team member helped another? Tell them how important it is for the other guy and how important this help was to the team's cohesion. Build positive constructive behavior through encouragement.

Praise, on the other hand, weakens the soul. It is harmful to your employee because it's impossible to break the praise into constructive behaviors that can be repeated. In fact research has found that a praised person may LOSE motivation because he or she is 'on top of the game' now - so there's no apparent reason to try anything else. Being wrong now can only harm the illusion of perfection created by the praise.

I personally had an encounter with the conflict between encouragement and praise in my first years as team leader. A gifted developer who worked in my team completed an assignment very successfully. I praised him like one would praise a king because I wanted him to understand the importance of his contribution. After a few weeks I noticed that he stopped making efforts and I falsely concluded that people should be neither encouraged nor praised - because I didn't understand the difference - and I thought that saying a good word, in general, can be dangerous. Only years after, when I learned to distinguish between encouragement and praise I solved this enigma for myself. In later years, when I internalized the essence of the matter – constructive encouragement became a central tool in building the team. For example, a developer created a feature that enabled better communication between two parts of a system. It was good work, so I told him his contribution would "assist the client in keeping his current communications equipment, save money, and leverage the user experience". "That is good work" I concluded. When I gave him that encouragement, I could see his eyes sparkle, and indeed I heard his enthusiasm. The teammate maintained high productivity because he KNEW he is important and that he was making an important contribution.

Encouragement is a tool that can be used in situations of failure, as well. It is not only used when a teammate succeeds. Praise is bound to success alone. Encouragement highlights the good in any situation; this is one of the beauties of encouragement. Remember that failure is a significant part of success. "Success is going from failure to failure without loss of enthusiasm" said Mr. Churchill. Encouragement is a great tool to drive people to enthusiasm.

Praise and encouragement are respectively related to extrinsic and intrinsic motivations. The two motivation types are opposite and complementary: Extrinsic motivation is generated by promise of reward or fear of punishment. Intrinsic motivation is generated by an internal drive to learn and to do things because of the matter itself.

Encouragement is a central tool in the Adlerian methodology because of the resulting intrinsic motivation. As team leaders, and as management in principle, we are interested in long term motivational engines that drive teams to work independently and efficiently towards their goals. The team must be able to recognize desired behaviors and reproduce these behaviors over and over again. Encouragement is the way to convey the constructive messages and lead the team to success.

Praise creates extrinsic motivation in that it is like a candy given for display of good behavior. Some claim that praise might also create an unhealthy dependency when an employee is constantly looking for the pat on the head for his good actions. We commonly hear employees complain their manager "didn't even say thanks". But "thanks" alone is not enough; a REASON for the thanks must be added. As a manager ask yourself: what was it about the employee's work for which you feel gratitude? What was the behavior you want them to replicate in the future as a pattern?

Not all extrinsic motivation is bad, but the Adlerian approach does not suggest tools that leverage this type of motivation. Driving employees with extrinsic motivation is, for example, launching a competition between employees, with promise of reward. Another (controversial) example is compensation plans that are calculated from achievement of SMART goals (Specific, Measureable, Assignable, Realistic, and Time-Based).

Equality in Value

You and your employees are all of equal human value. This is the starting point and underpins everything else we will be discussing here. Of course, you each have different roles in the team - but each teammate has equal value as a person. Reject hierarchical thinking where rank becomes a benchmark of human value. A manager isn't more valuable just because of his or her seniority.

Assertiveness and Boundaries

"Assertiveness is the quality of being self-assured and confident without being aggressive" [Wikipedia]. Being assertive is tightly bound to creating boundaries. Set your rules, set your boundaries, make decisions - and stand behind your decisions. Demand from your team what you demand of yourself. This is an important part of your job that provides a necessary service to your teammates. You'd be surprised at how important boundaries are for people. We don't like to admit this to ourselves - but boundaries make us feel safe. Knowing the boundaries makes us feel that something is stable in this world where "uncertainty is the only constant". A team leader must draw the boundaries for his team and be assertive enough to keep the team inside them.

Assertiveness is primarily expressed in speech. Keep the conversation relevant and keep the tones low and firm. Don't shout commands and generally don't be loud. Loudness is simply aggression - nothing more. Assertiveness is about standing behind your word. For example, several times, I requested programmers to check a problem in a system in a certain way, only to discover later that the developer used a shortcut. When that happened, I assertively requested that he or she carry out the investigation in the way I originally requested and politely explained the reasoning behind my decision. I did not open the decision for discussion, but requested results in 30 minutes - with a "thank you" at the end. There was no anger, no yelling, and no discouragement. An assertive request served as an action item with a deadline.

Assertiveness is used to give the team boundaries.

Once you have the form down - cultivating an environment of mutual respect based on an understanding that all are of equal value, yet setting limits and boundaries with assertiveness in order to fulfill your role as team leader, let's turn our attention to the content.

As a team leader, your interaction with your team will take place somewhere on the line between two extremes: autocracy and anarchy. Finding the right balance is key.

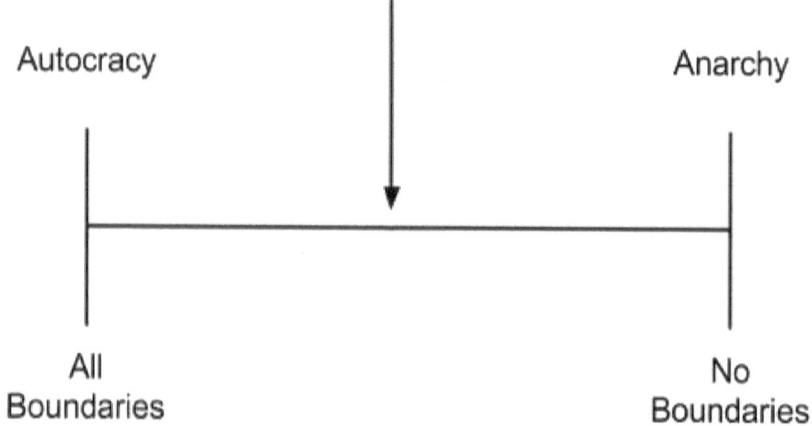

Autocracy

Anarchy

All
Boundaries

No
Boundaries

If you pull rank all the time and "tell people what to do", if you tell your people to do everything "your way or the highway" - then you're an autocrat. But if you let your team do whatever they want without boundaries, or if you overprotect them - even at the expense of the team's plan and goals - you're operating as an archetypical anarchist would. Your goal should be to build a healthy balance between the two.

Let's examine some common scenarios and suggest guidelines that can assist you in responding assertively.

Requesting something from an employee

When you have a request for someone in your team - don't shout it over to them above the crowd. It's disrespectful to shout commands to people. They're not your dogs. Get up from your seat, walk over to the person you want to address, kindly ask for their attention. After you have their attention, ask whatever you need.

Debating disagreement

When you disagree with an employee - never ever ever criticize. People are not doing things wrong because they are mean - but because they are human beings. You can disagree. As team leader you can be assertive about a different approach you want a teammate to take. Don't blame with using the word "You". Use the word "We" or "Us" instead. A teammate's action reflects the entire team's responsibility. A teammate's success is a team's success. A teammate's failure is a team's failure.

Educating

Sometimes people just act in an inappropriate manner. Determining if someone is acting inappropriately falls to you, the team leader. If it's important enough to you - educate teammates to behave according to your standards. Whatever the issue is - remember to base your conversation on the Adlerian principle of equality of value and respect. Be clear about the boundaries you set. Be assertive about those boundaries. It is ok for a teammate to disagree with you about your boundaries - but it is not ok to cross them. If a teammate does not play along - they will not be able to proceed as a member of your team.

Over Protectiveness

The opposite of setting boundaries is over protectiveness. When we spoil employees, give up on our principles because of an employee's stubbornness - we create a weak image and lose our control of the team. We'll call this "no borders".

Over protectiveness is a managerial syndrome where the manager feels uncomfortable demanding work from his or her employees. Some managers eventually take the team's assignments upon themselves – and that is very ineffective practice as a rule. It is not management and it weakens the team's connection to the product. Over protectiveness does not support the employee's need for significant contribution, and makes them feel redundant. This approach cannot survive as a long-term methodology.

If you find yourself at night working alone in the office, doing your team's work, it's an indication that you are over-protective. My recommendation would be: confront your team with the facts. Tell them that you can't take on everyone's assignments and that they need to show more involvement in the team activity.

Confronting your teammates and the team as a whole, setting boundaries for them - is central to creating team competency. I experienced several cases of teammates asking me for vacation near a deadline, or teammates who simply left early in times of pressure. Other times, teammates completed their OWN assignments but completely ignored the overall commitments of their team.

A disciplined team should run like a smooth engine: all parts working in harmony together to create movement under a set of rules. The overall output of the team is the responsibility of the team leader so you can't have team members doing just their own assignments in whatever way they think things should be done. You should rather have them working as a team complying to the rules determined by the team leader.

On a micro level, teammates might neglect technical responsibilities such as writing proper tests or cutting corners in the implementation. They might neglect their responsibility to communicate with the Product Owner or with the QA. You must insist on the process you want to see occurring by putting strong boundaries on the team, as far as the schedule allows.

You might be surprised to hear that boundaries are especially important for the more gifted developers. These champs are "all over the place"; they're very fast and they're very creative. If the gifted developers feel they don't have boundaries, they start developing an increasing feeling of over-significance, as they are not challenged enough. This will lead to anarchy. They will feel they know better than everyone around them. This is ineffective for the team and equally unsettling for the gifted teammate. Set the boundaries and then push the gifted individual further and harder inside these boundaries to challenge them according to their competency.

You must weigh the pros and cons of every decision but the most important thing is that you must empirically test what you can ask from an employee and what you can't. My manager told me once about a certain employee that "you can't demand of him what he can't supply". In this particular case, I did try to push the employee to do things beyond his comfort zone, but encountered too much resistance. I weighed the pros and cons and decided eventually that the benefits of his performance are greater than those I will have should he leave the team or get demotivated. I let go of some of my demands in this case. This approach is reinforced by many articles that claim it is better to develop and focus on an employee's strengths rather than trying to improve their weaknesses.

Events Interpretations Emotions Reactions (EIER)

The EIER framework is an extremely strong thought framework to control anger and conflict. Simply put, it is a tool that helps us listen, understand, and maintain positive interactions without getting upset.

An event is not objective; it is conceived subjectively according to the individuals' life's view. When a child throws things - a parent might think the child is deliberately trying to harm his surroundings - or oppose the parent. However, children generally don't do things AGAINST their parents - but only FOR themselves. It's a paradigm shifting insight that allows people to interpret events and react in a whole new way.

Think about your employees. They don't control anything. They don't determine the project, they don't determine the priorities. Sometime they don't even determine the design. They might have every reason to feel insignificant, an emotion which can easily lead to unhealthy thoughts. Employees would almost NEVER behave in unconstructive ways with explicit bad intentions against their company or manager. They will, though, act in unconstructive ways because of their internal emotional conflicts. Meaning - they won't act against you - but for themselves.

When you are engaged in an event of conflict or confrontation - you interpret what you experience. Your interpretation overflows into emotions. These emotions drive you to react.

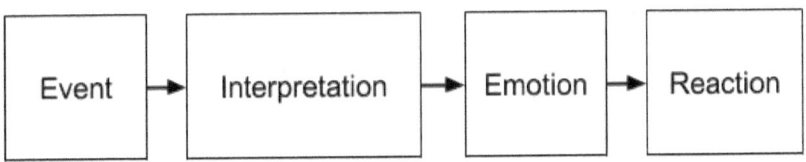

Our emotional control is bound to the interpretation. Let me give you an example from parenting. On a Monday morning at 6:30 AM, my 2.5 year old girl wanted a hot bottle of her baby food (hot water with a milk powder). In order to create it, I poured some cold water into the bottle with intention of putting the bottle in the microwave to warm the water. My daughter got upset because she wanted a hot bottle - but saw me making a cold one. Without hesitation she reached out with her little arm, grabbed the bottle, and poured it all over the kitchen countertop.

What would you do as a parent?

It would be a normal reaction to yell in fury or punish the child because a parent interpreted the child's act as aggressiveness against the parent. However, if we seek out the child's motivation, looking for why he did this FOR him or herself, we can access other emotions and elicit a different reaction and a positive end to the overall scene. My daughter had obviously been very disappointed when she didn't see her hot bottle. She was also probably very hungry and lacked the tools to help herself prepare her meal. She was NOT achieving her goal and became very disappointed and quite helpless. I understood this and was able to show empathy. I quietly explained to my daughter that the cold water was only the first part of the preparation and that we would clean the mess together and start over. My daughter seemed pleased by the explanation. The situation was somewhat of a defining moment for me as a parent: I learned that seeing things from the child's perspective enables me to react in ways that will encourage the child to learn from the undesired behavior, as opposed to getting into a destructive conflict.

These are lessons you can use with your team.

A developer in my team had completed his assignment, so he decided independently to update the QA environment. However, the QA environment must be sterile for testing, with no developer intervention. When I approached the developer to discuss the status of his assignment I discovered he broke the rule and indeed installed software parts on that QA environment.

What would you do as a manager?

It would be completely reasonable to get upset at the developer and accuse him of cutting corners as well as breaking team rules. I decided to investigate the developer's motivation, taking into account the Adlerian axiom that no one does anything "against" others but only "for" themselves. By taking this approach, I found that in this particular case there was no harm to the testing environment. As the company's QA professional no longer worked with us and we had a tight deadline, it had actually been a good idea to alter the QA environment. The developer's intentions were good, and his rationalization helpful. The overall situation ended positively, with the project benefiting from the developer's unorthodox input. The QA environment rule was respectfully discussed and understood by the team member. Generally, people will push boundaries to seek independence. Let them take the lead. Let them become independent. It is a longed for goal to have independent and proactive teammates. It is good management.

Independence 0% → 100%

Your teammates start their journey in the team completely clueless. In addition to having nothing to offer in the beginning, they are a burden to everyone else. Your goal as Team Leader is to have every team member operate at 100% independence in the shortest time possible. Team member independence assists you in achieving your goals and adds to the employees' sense of contribution and value. Remember what it felt like to start a job in a new environment? You felt redundant. That you were "leeching" on everybody else. When you started you needed help - so you took others' time - and their concentration from their own assignments. Remember the feeling of not completely understanding the domain in which the product operates? The employee will always try to bridge the gap between his helplessness and his desire to fit in and succeed. The team leader should intentionally leverage the effort and aim towards a 100% independent employee.

When the team is 100% independent, you have an additional benefit of being able to drive people to excellence. Increasing your team's quality and scope relies on the independence of team members.

When a team member is 100% on top of his or her game - you can broaden the scope of your demands, thus enhancing the team's achievements.

"They" say: a good manager can leave the office from time to time and the team can handle it independently. A mediocre manager can't leave the office because everybody is dependent upon him. A bad manager can leave the office for good and everything will just work the same... Aim to be a good manager.

Letting Go

In order to give your team members independence and confidence - just let go. This is one of the hardest things for a manager to do. It is even harder for perfectionists. But it's the only way to devise an independent team.

So how do you let go? Adler offers a tool called "Reasonable and Logical Consequences". Adler suggests that to enable independence, the leader should provide instruction and then step back to let employees confront the results of their actions. "Letting go" applies to many areas of your daily work. For example, letting go can come in the form of delegating production problems. A problem will arise from a user and you delegate a team member to lead the support on your side. Another instance could be during routine development cycles; you can allow a developer to come up with his or her own bold design as a solution. Similarly, you can give a developer overall responsibility for a subject, and let him or her "run free" to handle the case. Of course, if you see your team crashing a production system to the wall, about to cause huge problems with major financial consequences - you need to catch them before they fall. Crashing your company is not what we're aiming for. We do want to offer your team challenges and allow them to accumulate experience.

Before adopting this approach, pay careful attention to your own company culture. If your company's culture tolerates failure - it is easier to let go. If there isn't any tolerance for mistakes, then tread more carefully when providing your teammates their independence. Decide the best balance between striving for independent team members and clashing with company culture.

Belong, Significant, Capable

Adler teaches us that to build a child's confidence; the three necessary steps are to make them feel loved, significant, and capable. Being loved is the most fundamental human need and fuels the feeling of belonging that is at the very heart of confidence and personal success.

How do we translate this into work spaces? How can we provide for our employees' emotional needs in a completely constructive way? The most basic thing we can do is create an environment where you and others show appreciation and in which all members are kind to one another. This provides the sense of belonging that a person needs so much.

Feeling you belong is not enough though. A person needs to know that he is significant to everyone else. Think about how it feels when you know someone relies on you for something. This feeling connects us to our environment and encourages us to struggle for what needs to be done. You want your employees to feel this emotion. They need to know that they have a place among the others and that the team relies on them. According to Adler, this is a basic human need. As such, showing someone that they are needed will help motivate them to do their best while being loyal to their genuine needs.

Feeling you belong and that people rely on you is still just another building block, however. In order to build confidence, according to Adler, you also need to know that you are capable. If people we appreciate rely on us, but we are incapable of supplying what is required - we experience a sense of failure. Employees have varying strengths and weaknesses. If we push them too much where they are incapable - we run the risk of ruining their confidence in themselves. We should set high, but achievable and tangible goals. We should support our employees with an environment that drives towards enhancing capabilities so they can eventually achieve more than they think they can achieve today.

Contribution and usefulness are important foundations of building confidence and high perception of self. Encourage your team members when they make contributions and stress the usefulness of their actions.

Responsibility

Managers have responsibilities by definition, developers don't. Yet, as a manager, it may be a good practice to give your developers targeted responsibility. Giving your developers responsibility for something (other than completing their tasks) makes them feel valuable and feel their contribution to the effort. In the Agile methodology of Lean Software Development, which we'll discuss at length later on, there is an entire approach related to responsibility called 'responsibility-based planning and control' [Poppendieck].

However, be careful not to overload your developers with responsibility. Developers are not built for managerial tasks because they need to focus on code lines and system architecture. Good software development requires undivided attention. It is hard to change hats. Developers may get sloppy in taking ownership of a business goal - and therefore get disappointed by their lack of capability to fulfill what is expected of them. Additionally, developers don't attend all the business meetings and that gives them a partial image of a business goal. Partial information causes bad decisions.

Taking the Initiative - avoid "reaction based"

When managing a team, be proactive. Don't wait for things to happen by themselves or go wrong. For example, don't wait for your team to just 'get along' with each other or befriend each other. You can start lecture evenings with pizza, invite everyone for lunch or organize a video game night. If you have a team member with whom you have a genuine connection - you can invite him or her and spouse for dinner with you and your spouse (do check your corporate ethics on this one). On the professional side - suggest ideas for technical improvements, software tools you want to build or try, ideas for prototypes using some unique technologies, suggest hackathons, invite the team for lectures outside the team. Anything goes. What doesn't go is sitting idly by and only managing assignments.

Setting Expectations

We are only upset by events that did not rise to our expectations. Proactively setting expectations is a critical step in managing your team.

There are two types of expectations. Our expectations from employees and their expectations from us.

We must be clear to our employees about what is expected of them. Without that, employees will not have any compass to know what they should be doing. And you will only get upset because there is little chance your teammate is meeting your unstated expectations. If a developer is considered a "lead developer" he or she might be expected to be a guide to the other developers in addition to their development tasks. This isn't in the job definition - and the lead developer might not independently think of taking this on. If we set expectations together with the developer - then everything can proceed as agreed.

We must also be clear about setting the employees' expectations from us. We need to be clear about our goals and our vision. We also need to be clear about what's going to happen today, what's going to happen this week, and what is going to happen this month. Be very careful NOT to give false information or set expectations of something that you're not sure is going to happen. Not meeting expectations causes disappointment which in turn may impact motivation. Of course, things change. Always. When you need to react to that change, you will probably fail to meet SOME expectations in your team. That's ok. But communicate about the change and let them know to expect it.

Manager-Employee Time

Taking some time to privately speak and spend time with employees is important. Employees need this time because they need to be confident in their place in the team. They need to be heard. They need to feel they have a real connection to their manager and that they are not disappearing in the loudness of the day between assignments and other team members. Later in this book I will describe a bi-weekly meeting between you and the employees.

Disturbing Behaviors

Many time, employees exhibit disturbing behaviors that can't be directly explained. For example, an employee in my team wrote some code, which another employee erased entirely, changing the whole implementation. The first employee was disproportionately outraged; he could not even sit at his desk and just walked out of the office. It may seem that he was angry about what had happened - but I believe something deeper was at play. A team member who is confident in his place, who knows he's respected, who feels significant and know that he's contributing to the team - will NEVER react in such a disproportionate manner to an event of this kind. In this case, I was responsible for not creating the required emotional safety net (it was my first period as team leader...)

Disturbing behaviors are almost always a result of an underlying process that should be analyzed with psychological tools. People do things for themselves not against others. These kind of behaviors are a result of people trying to compensate for emotional gaps that otherwise don't find solutions. They feel driven to a behavior that is out of line or out of common sense.

It will serve you to get to the root cause of any disturbing behavior you encounter. Don't get pulled into struggles with people displaying this type of behavior and don't respond to it. **Concentrate on the person - not on the act.**

Power struggles

Power struggles are sometimes inevitable. They may occur between you and team members, or between the team members themselves.

There are two seasons, and it will serve you to distinguish between them: struggle season and peace season. When in struggle, education doesn't work. People don't listen, don't want to listen, and won't want to learn. When in peaceful times - people are calm, pay attention and can be reasoned with. The argument you always win - is an argument that never occurred. Don't get into pointless arguments when emotions are running high. Wait for everything to calm down and then proceed to personal meetings and set expectations for future events. Use the past to construct reason as a basis for the future.

Power struggles and disturbing behaviors are both a result of emotional gaps. If they occur often - you may have an underlying issue in your team that needs to be addressed.

Managerial Consensus

You and your manager must be on the same page in your approach to the team. If your manager reverses your decisions or manages your team members in a way that opposes your approach - you will lose grip on your team - and your influence will shrink. Make sure your manager understands this principle and explicitly ask him or her to raise objections and ask for changes during one-to-one conversations with you - not in front of the team.

Getting into conflicts with your manager in front of your team can be very uncomfortable and very confusing for team members. When cracks appear in the thing that is their stability - team members lose confidence in their assumptions and thus lose confidence in their (relative) place.

Listening & Empathizing

Listening is incredibly important. People are different. They think differently, they talk differently. Everyone has his or her own pace. In order to listen, you need to respect the other's pace and wait for the other to complete what they want to express.

Sometime people just want to be heard. They don't always want advice, and they don't always want to hear what you think about what they're saying. They just need someone to talk to, to share with, to be part of what they are experiencing.

Empathize with other's difficulties. Not everything that is easy for you is easy for someone else. Some people have trouble in dealing with change. Some people have trouble dealing with certain types of assignments. Be empathic to other people's challenges and most importantly respect their personal challenges.

To practice 'listening' do the following exercise: Sit with a friend or your spouse and ask to be told a story about something important to them. The story should be only a few minutes long and about an issue or topic that you don't usually discuss with that person. Listen carefully to the story. Afterwards - repeat the main issue raised by the speaker. Say what you think THEY think about it (not what YOU think about it). This is a listening simulation that helps us understand what it means to really listen to the other without involving our own agenda and perception.

Seniority & Competition

Senior employees usually share an unwritten assumption that their seniority affords them more privileges than other team members. While it's important to respect employees' achievements over the years - new employees are often as productive as their senior counterparts.

There may be issues between the two groups: senior employees may become competitive or shut themselves out when feeling threatened by new colleagues, while newer employees may get competitive if they feel they're being patronized by senior teammates and are not recognized by their manager.

Your job is to make both groups feel valued and remove the competition between them. Give the seniors confidence that they are recognized for their past achievements and relied on for future achievement and team collaboration. In parallel, provide new employees with confidence that their achievements are recognized in absolute terms rather than by unhealthy comparison to a senior's accumulated work.

Managerial Vision and Employee Development

Everyone needs to know that they have a future so that they can be confident in the present. When an individual's future is unclear he/she can't function as well because they worry all the time. Make sure your employees have a future to aim for: a personal development to look forward to.

Money is a primary incentive for some people. In these cases, make sure they see a future in the form of raises and compensations. Some people seek promotions. For this group, make sure they have a career path plan from HR. Some people want to improve professionally so comply with their need of education, professional courses, guidance, or challenge them accordingly.

You need to have a vision for your employees. Think about each of your employees - how do you imagine them growing? how do you imagine them evolving? how do you imagine them getting better?

Take your insights and align them with the employees themselves. Don't try to invent for them what they want to be when they grow up. Let them think about that on their own. When they give you an answer - do everything that you can to build a plan to support their aspirations.

I believe that if a team member's aspiration is to eventually leave the team, they should be supported in that decision. Your job in this case would be to make sure an infrastructure is prepared to allow the inevitable turnover, which supports the team member in building him or herself for his or her next challenge under an agreed schedule through agreed goals. I would first suggest a fix for the current situation and see if something could be done to keep them in the team. However, if there is no solution, then it is your moral duty as a leader to develop your employee according to his or her own ambitions. This attitude will have trickle-down effect because it will be inspiring and comforting to other team members who see the great respect you afford each individual, even when not necessarily in your own best interest.

Tolerance as an Innovation Driver

Tolerance of others drives individuals towards creativity. This is backed by research. Facebook's past motto was "Move fast and break things". This corporate statement drove employees to TRY without fear of consequences. If we don't show tolerance to failure - we will not achieve major success. Without creativity and innovation we can only achieve incremental change that rides on the existing status quo. Failure is a natural part of success. Think of a child learning to walk. Think of a chef at the beginning of his or her way.

Evolution of business is commonly divided into 4 types, 3 of which are activities that involve innovation and creativity:

Creativity in product features

Creativity in product adaptation will open new markets. Creativity in product features will diversify our user base. Creativity in features and markets will bring us to blue ocean innovation.

Blue Ocean Innovation is the Holy Grail in business. It's called "Blue Ocean" because it's a part of the sea where the sharks have not yet shown up and turned it red....

Innovation starts with ideas. Ideas are like small plants that need nurturing to grow. It's easy to destroy them when they're young because they are weak and small. But if we nurture them correctly - they will grow to become beautiful and fruitful. The famous story of 3M's sticky notes is a good example. Glue that doesn't adhere seemed ridiculous and irrelevant at first. The idea was misunderstood at the beginning - but nobody dared to kill it out of respect to the inventor. Now, it is a huge business with billions of dollars in income and revenue.

Part II

The Agile Team Leader

Introduction

This chapter is about your workflow -

WHAT needs to be done,
    WHEN things should get done,
        HOW things should be done,
            WHO should do it -
                ... and most importantly **WHY**.

In this chapter we'll introduce Agile methodologies that will help you manage the workflow in your team.

The term 'Agile' is VERY general. We'll explain later exactly what it is, but when you give it a second look you'll discover that in fact - Agile doesn't have almost anything to do specifically with software. Agile is a set of principles that can be used in your home with your kids, in government, in schools, in the army, in negotiations, in general business affairs and in any other place where systems are dynamic and human interaction is important.

Many try to compare Agile to Lean methodology - but it is like comparing apples to oranges. Lean is a specific methodology for manufacturing processes - in our case, the manufacturing of software. Agile is a set of high level principles for a dynamic environment with a lot of human interaction.

The bottom line is: if you're doing Lean - you're doing Agile. Just don't force yourself into squeezing these two methodologies together.

Agile

Agile methodologies are now an inseparable part of software development. If you want to manage a development process well - you have to work Agile.

Agile methodologies are a result of empirical failures in software projects. Software projects were originally executed in "Waterfall" methodology just like in any other classical engineering discipline: Requirements were gathered, a design was made, later the design was implemented by developers, the QA and the client would verify the validity of the project and eventually the project would enter the maintenance stage.

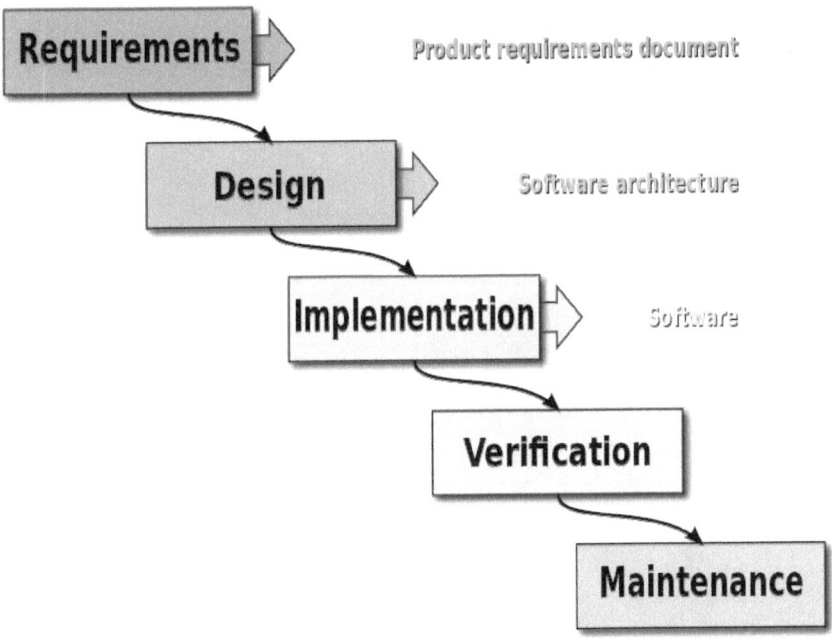

[Source: Wikipedia]

The waterfall model doesn't work. Software is too dynamic. The requirements can never really be complete at the beginning of the project lifecycle. Software can fundamentally change during the project lifecycle unlike other traditional engineering projects such as civil engineering: When you build a bridge - it stays a bridge. It never transforms into scalable multithreaded bridge with zero response time...

Agile grew out of some smart folks from the software industry sitting down to discuss some of the problems they were encountering with the industry. It took them about 30 years to come to a conclusion - but eventually they converged to "Agile Development" which is an umbrella term for all the methodologies that are practiced in today's software industry.

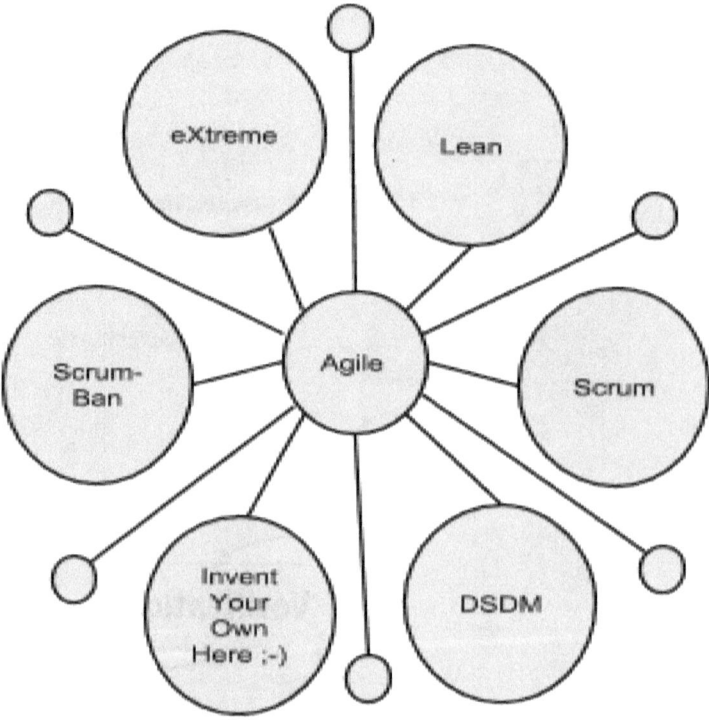

Agile gives high value to personal communication between team members and with other collaborators in the project. It appreciates working software more than synthetic project milestones. It urges the customer's or product-leader's involvement in the development process. Most importantly - it is adaptive to change. In their own words, the Agile Software Development Manifesto (the entire copyright text has to be taken as a whole) –

We are uncovering better ways of developing
software by doing it and helping others do it.
Through this work we have come to value:

Individuals and interactions over processes and tools
Working software over comprehensive documentation
Customer collaboration over contract negotiation
Responding to change over following a plan

Kent Beck	James Grenning	Robert C. Martin
Mike Beedle	Jim Highsmith	Steve Mellor
Arie van Bennekum	Andrew Hunt	Ken Schwaber
Alistair Cockburn	Ron Jeffries	Jeff Sutherland
Ward Cunningham	Jon Kern	Dave Thomas
Martin Fowler	Brian Marick	

So, what does this give us other than vague statements?

The principles of Agile software development spawned frameworks that help us order the work. Scrum, eXtreme, Scrum-Kanban, Lean, Scrum-Ban - these are a few frameworks that are popular in the industry. Applying these rules feels like playing a game. For the most part, there is much resemblance to a game - only with the following **acute warning**:

> Although there are many rule-sets today - the most important thing you need to understand is that they are all practices that **you need to interpret yourself**. Never take them as-is. You must be very skeptical and read everything with examining eyes. Some of the worst practices are a result of misinterpreted or abused Agile rules that are forced on inadequate circumstances. You can make up your own rules to whatever fits you.

Although Agile methodologies are subject to interpretation - make sure you do make some principal rules and stand behind them. The last thing a team needs is a confused team leader that changes the methodology all the time or doesn't stand behind the agreed set of rules.

Scrum

Scrum is one example of an Agile methodology. An interpretation of the Agile manifesto, It is easy to relate to because it is very well-defined. Its strength is in its fixed rule set.

Scrum is a simple game. It organizes your team so you can build new products or enhance existing products. However, Scrum is inadequate for support teams or bugs fixes. For these you can use Lean, Scrum with Kanban or Scrumban or any other fluent life cycle based methodology.

How Do You Go About Developing a New Product?

The Players ("Who")
First, you need a **Team** to build it. The team must have multidisciplinary capabilities; they must be a multifunctional team. The key members would probably be a backend developer, an android developer, an iOS developer and a UX designer. Recruit professionals with each of the skillsets required to build the product. The ideal team is "self-organized", which means they're able to communicate with each other and commit to requirements. The team should be capable of delivering commitments.

Sometimes a team will get stuck - that's where you come in as team leader. Actually, in Scrum, you are called "**Scrum Master**" - but that's just semantics. The team leader is responsible to make sure that nobody gets stuck. Getting stuck could be a developer drifting away from his or her assignment because of false prioritization, refactoring that gets out of control, or a million other things. Another example of getting stuck could be real technical issues that arise and that the developer can't make work. Sometimes other impediments unrelated to a team member can arise: servers can be down, licenses for tools must be acquired and knowledge might be missing. These impediments should all be removed by the team leader so everyone on the team can make the schedule.

What will the team and team leader build? What should they build first? What is the overall plan? All this depends on the **Product Owner**'s requirements and prioritization. The product owner represents the client and maintains direct interface with him or her. The Product Owner commits to goals agreed with the client - and is responsible for the team delivering those goals. So - does the team leader call the product owner "boss"? In some way - they should, but they don't. That's because Scrum and Agile are built around emotional values that assume greatness of men and zero ego.

Zero ego? Yes! Team leaders or teams with an agenda that is not transparent to the product owner will not be working according to priority and eventually harm the project. In organizations in which the product owner is weak and development does whatever they feel like - things get messy really quickly.

Here's a checklist for you to quickly see if you're getting the scrum roles right -

Team

1. Sized 3-9 individuals
2. Multidisciplinary / Multifunctional - does everything from design to delivery
3. Self-organizing
4. Communicate well with each other
5. Commit to tasks by themselves

Scrum Master

1. Focused on releasing impediments for the team
2. Servant Leader (see reference list)
3. Make sure Scrum meetings (a.k.a "events", "ceremonies") occur

Product Owner

1. High EQ (Emotional Quotient)
2. Communicates with the client
3. Communicates with the team and the Scrum Master
4. Represents the client
5. Prioritizes tasks
6. Has the final responsibility for the product as a whole

The Backlog ("What")

Let's build a product! Where do we start? What is more important and what is less important? A list of assignments is created and prioritized. The Product Owner is responsible for defining the exact content of the assignments. In Scrum, they're called **User Stories**. The User Story should be carefully written and even more carefully read by the team. It defines what needs to be done. It represents the common understanding agreed between all the stakeholders in the project - from developer to client. In Scrum (opposite to Lean) you should NEVER start the development before EVERYTHING is understood and finalized in the User Story. The User Story is the reference for the developer, for the UX designer, for the QA, and eventually for the client. Don't underestimate the importance of this. As team leader you MUST insist on this requirement firmly and strongly: you don't start the development before the User Story is complete and understood.

The single and complete collection of User Stories along with **ANY OTHER** work item that the team needs to work on is known as **The Backlog**. Commonly, what you'll find in the backlog is -

1. User Stories
2. Investigation tasks
3. Proof of concept tasks
4. Maintenance
5. Bugs

Let's focus on a User Story since it is a central piece in the Scrum methodology. A User Story is minimally comprised of the following

attributes –

Title: One line to describe the goal of the User Story
Description: A detailed description of the User Story
Definition of Done (DoD): The criteria that will determine that the User Story is complete
Priority: The relative priority in the backlog
Assigned To: The team member committed to delivering the User Story
Estimation: How much time (or "points") it will take to complete the User Story
State: Represents the state of the User Story e.g. "In Development", "Done", etc.

Following the list above, any work item other than a User Story should be comprised of similar attributes.

What should the team do first? That depends on the prioritization of the backlog. The Product Owner will generally take either of the following prioritization approaches -

Motivation 1: Reduce the risk of the project as soon as possible
Resulting Approach: Prioritize the harder work items

Motivation 2: Show progress to the client as soon as possible
Resulting Approach: Prioritize the easier work items

Scrum Project Lifecycle ("When")

After we decide **what** needs to be done and **who** needs to do it, let's schedule **when** we're going to do it. We'll start with a basic work item such as a User Story. At the core of the life cycle a User Story is simply a "Ready → In Progress → Done" flow:

But how does a User Story become "Ready"? Who puts it in this category? The Product Owner puts great effort in defining the required tasks and into further refining the "definition of done" which is the criteria that will later determine the successful completion or failure of the development. In Scrum, all the involved participants are summoned for a special meeting called "**Planning**". The participant are

1. The Product Owner
2. The Scrum Master
3. The specific team members responsible for implementing the User Story - including the QA

Some question the QA's involvement in the planning meeting. Trust me on this one - the QA MUST be present. QAs have a special view on the system and often offer the best remarks regarding the risks and effects of adding new features to systems. Additionally, QAs will test the feature in extreme scenarios and therefore must be acquainted with the intimate details of a task.

At the Planning Meeting, the Product Owner will introduce the User Story to the participants. The participants ask questions and investigate the details of the planned development. The product owner answers questions to the best of his or her ability and will refine the requirements until the team is certain they understand everything and can start work. Let's take a new look at our workflow now –

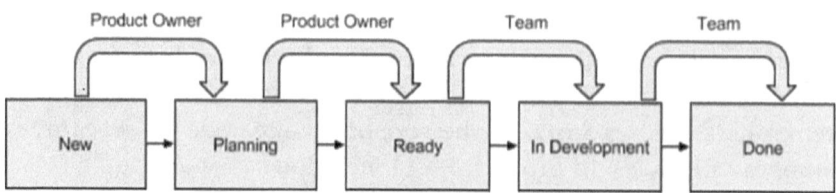

Ok. We reached the end of the workflow and the work item is "done". What happens now? Before going to production, the Product Owner meets the team on the other side of development and confirms the deliverable is indeed as was intended. This is called an **Acceptance Test**. During the Acceptance Test the Product Owner approves the deliverable or sends it back to development. An Acceptance Test is executed on an installed environment, not on a development machine, because there are special conditions on the development machines that may enable the item to pass the acceptance test when it would fail miserably on a production machine. Let's add the Acceptance Test to the workflow.

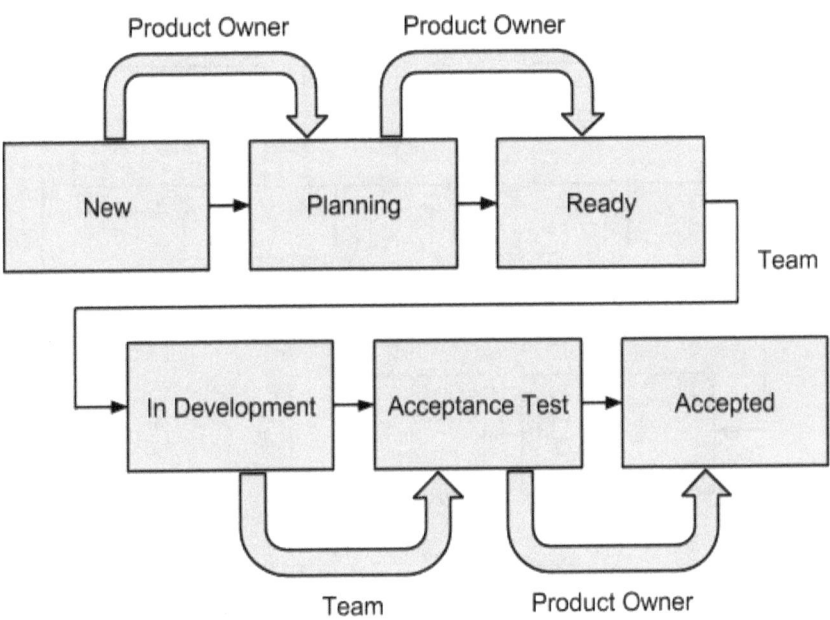

So where does the QA come in on the workflow? Is it part of the development process or should it be done after the Acceptance Test? Acceptance Tests and QA check altogether different parameters so each organization will need to determine when it is most effective to introduce the QA process. QA plays out extreme scenarios, while Acceptance Tests ensure the work product fulfills the requirements of "Definition of Done". Some decide to perform QA tests before Acceptance Tests to save Product Owner time and to save an acceptance cycle. On the other hand - a QA's time might also be expensive and the process usually takes much longer than an Acceptance Test. You need to decide on a workflow that fits YOUR needs. For our purposes, let's put the QA state after the Acceptance Test:

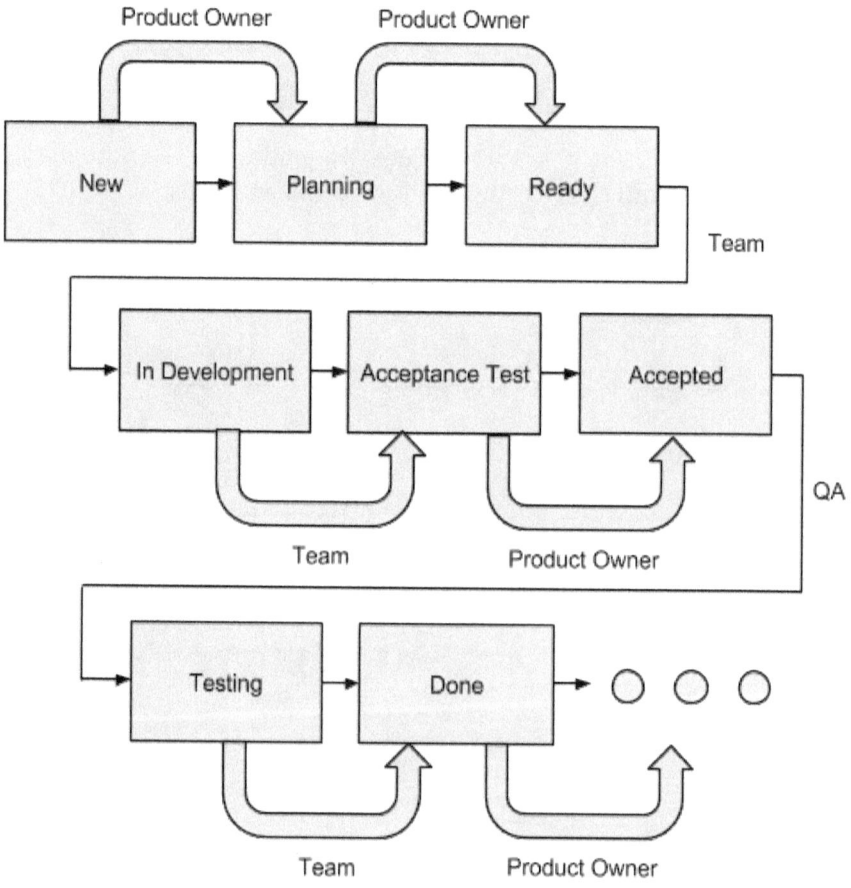

Examine the final stage of the User Story. It is given to the Product Owner along with other User Stories. The results would eventually be displayed to the customer. These activities are all part of the Product Owner's domain.

Planning meetings are actually not about one User Story - but include a broader discussion on the entire backlog. In the planning meeting the committed parties will agree on ALL the items that need to be put in the "pipeline". According to Scrum, the length of the pipeline is about 1-4 weeks and is defined as an **Iteration** or **Sprint**.

The work items that the parties select for the iteration are collectively known as the **Iteration Backlog**, which is set up before the iteration begins. In "The Scrum Guide" by Ken Schwaber and Jeff Sutherland,

planning is comprised of two parts:
1. Discussion of which work items should be included in the sprint backlog
2. Discussion on the design and implementation of each of the work items.

From my experience, it is not possible to "tie up all loose ends" in one planning meeting. In many cases, issues come up. For example, the architecture needs to be designed at greater length, or the highest priority work items need to be better defined by the product owner. Therefore a planning meeting might have a consecutive planning meeting; the agreed iteration backlog will be determined only after all planning meetings. The same article ("The Scrum Guide") suggests an 8 hour planning meeting for each 4 weeks of iteration (e.g. 4 hours per 2 weeks iteration).

Let's sketch the work flow:

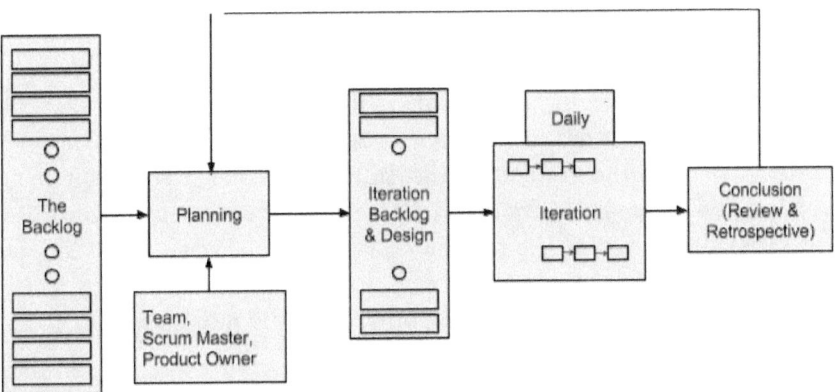

Let's focus on the last two boxes - the iteration and the conclusion.

The iteration length is 1-4 weeks. During this time - the work items in the iteration backlog progress in the pipeline through the states from "Ready" to "Done". In Scrum, the team would meet every day in a **Daily Standup Meeting**. The meeting is limited to 15 minutes. In this important meeting the team members discuss 3 issues only -

1. What they accomplished yesterday
2. What they plan to accomplish today

3. Any impediments that are stopping them from accomplishing their commitments

This is an update meeting - not an in-depth investigation on impediments. The Scrum Master takes notes on the impediments raised. I always prefer having the Product Owner on board. The Product Owner can usually solve impediments better than anyone in the business domain - and most importantly a Product Owner can provide critical information. Sometimes developers get themselves into unrequired pitfalls by imagining fictional client requirements that are not actually needed. The Product Owner straightens this up instantaneously saving hours to days of effort.

Theoretically, after the Iteration is done - the players gather for two concluding meetings. Some of the content of these two meetings are redundant with other contents in the Scrum methodology, so commonly you'll find that one or both of these meetings is skipped. But here they are, so you know about them and if you choose to, can skip them with foreknowledge.

The first closing meeting is the **Sprint Review** meeting where Scrum players and any other participant, such as the client, meet and collaborate over the results of the Iteration. Work items that may have passed acceptance tests and QA - can be reopened if they are not satisfactory to the client. The collaborators discuss the state of the backlog, reviewing what has been done and what still needs to be done and roughly agreeing on the contents of the next iteration.

The second closing meeting is the **Sprint Retrospective** meeting where Scrum players (without any other stakeholders) collaborate on the Scrum process itself. Personally, I ask team members to come prepared to this meeting with 2 issues they wish to keep in the process and 2 issues they would like to improve. The conclusions of the meeting are then shaped into action items that are implemented in the next iteration, thus allowing the process to improve more and more during each iteration.

This is our short introduction to Scrum methodology. I invite you to read the references on the subject. Remember that everyone gives different interpretations to the same Scrum theory - and that you must not take the rules as rules - but as recommendations. For example, I found that calling the Product Owner for a Pre-Acceptance Test at the development computer can save hours of work for everyone. Just before the developer checks-in the code - the Product Owner is summoned to express his or her opinion on the results. This kind of meeting would not be documented anywhere in Scrum theory - but as you can assume - it is VERY efficient and improves the Scrum process vastly. As you work with Scrum methodology, see what works for you - and implement it, leaving out the parts that are not useful.

Scrum Religion

Some people who promote the methodology claim it needs to be used religiously, exactly as it is written, in its entirety. They don't believe you can "pick and choose" parts. Scrum is not math. It's not a religion. Nothing in it should be referred to as sacred. I do agree that misinterpreted Scrum, and partially understood Scrum, can be as dangerous as any other partially understood theory. Make sure you get Scrum as a whole - that you understand the entire theory and learn the whole methodology - and then judge the changes you would like to implement with proper understanding of pros and cons.

Summary

For easy reference remember these simple parts of Scrum:

Roles -
1. Scrum Master
2. Product Owner
3. Team

Events
1. Sprint Planning
2. Daily Scrum Meeting
3. Sprint Review
4. Sprint Retrospective

Artifacts
1. Product Backlog
2. Sprint Backlog
3. Incremental Release

Lean Software Development

Introduction

Lean Software Development is a software development process. Starting with a short retrospective on software development will help clarify the ideas. Like any process, software development can hide inefficiencies. These inefficiencies are known as wastes. "Lean Software Development" is a theoretical framework that reveals and confronts these inefficiencies. The framework was initiated through a series of books authored by Mary and Tom Poppendieck, which appeared alongside the "Lean Startup" movement, led by Eric Ries. Their important research and activity clarified the inefficiencies and enabled the establishment of a set of principles to handle them.

Here is the full list of the wastes that may be found in a software project:

1. Partially done work
2. Extra Features
3. Relearning
4. Handoffs
5. Task Switching
6. Delays
7. Defects

Lean Software Development is an adaptation of the Toyota Production System - an industry-proven methodology for manufacturing processes. The theory relies on well-established industrial engineering principles, including those adapted from the Theory of Constraints (ToC) by the Israeli business management guru Eliyahu M. Goldratt.

The Production Line

At its core, a software development process resembles a production line. Look at the User Story life cycle again - it is a chain of stations just like in a manufacturing plant. The User Story flows through the pipeline from inception to production. If the work item gets stuck somewhere in the pipeline - it becomes waste. Just like a production line where material becomes stuck, like inventory on the production floor, work items that didn't get out of the production line are a problem. In Lean Software Development - the inventory is unfinished work.

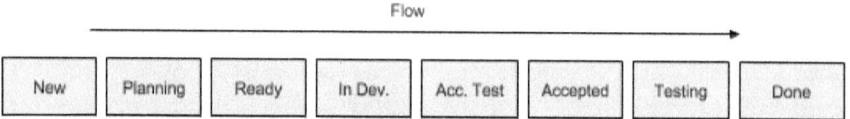

Noted by Corey Ladas, the entire Lean approach rests on two axioms that Scrum made us believe are a "given truth" regarding any problem (they're not...). The Lean axioms are -

- "Axiom #1: It is possible to divide the work into small value-adding increments that can be independently scheduled.
- Axiom #2: It is possible to develop any value-adding increment in a continuous flow from requirement to deployment"

If either of the axioms don't exist in your environment - you can't use Lean. If you can't break the problem into small deployable chunks - you can't do the magic we're talking about here. Note that you also can't do Scrum if these two criteria don't exist, so don't take it out specifically on Lean... There might be a missing axiom here which is: there must be a pipeline in the first place. Not all development teams uniformly work in a single, well-defined pipeline that can be optimized, like in a manufacturing plant. We'll leave the last point for the accumulated experience that will take shape in the coming years.

Interpreting this pipeline through Lean bring us to the seven principles that comprise the Lean Software Development methodology.

Principle #1: Eliminate Waste

Let's examine the wastes and comments on each waste through the eyes of Lean Software Development.

Partially done work: An assignment that starts but is never completed. A work item with a partial definition of done. Lack of understanding of the business domain. Lack of understanding of deployment considerations. All these, and more, require investment of energy on things that simply don't return value.

Extra Features: Building features that nobody needs is the central problem that the "Lean Startup" addresses. Lean defines the Minimum Viable Product (MVP) and Minimum Viable Feature (MVF) as distillations of the most important requirements that must be delivered. When the pipeline produces features that nobody will use – it is wasted effort. The minimum requirements that forge the required functionality of the product should be the highest (and only) priority of the pipeline. They should be delivered to the client as quickly as possible.

In Lean terms - any extra features are over-production.

Startups in general are the most likely to ignore the MVP approach, usually to their own detriment. While large software shops create some waste, small startups repeatedly decide to create extra features that nobody wants; this may result in the termination of the entire company.

Relearning: Software is complex. It has a lot of moving parts and there is a lot to remember -by both the development party and the client. Clients will often forget what they ordered. Details get lost. When software is not delivered quickly enough, people have the same conversations over and over and make decisions that conflict earlier decisions. Relearning causes us to lose time on work items that should have been done in one small quickly delivered chunk.

Handoffs: When one colleague hands work off to another, there will necessarily be a loss of tacit information that creates waste. The

Poppendiecks compare this to teaching a child how to ride a bike over and over again from square one. Here are 4 recommendations for avoiding handoff waste:

1. "Reduce the number of handoffs"
2. Build cross functional teams so "people can teach each other how to ride"
3. "Communicate and document heavily"
4. "Release partial or preliminary work for consideration and feedback as soon as possible and as often as practical."

Task Switching: Software development requires concentration. This is one of the main reasons a team leader usually should not delve into a development assignment. From my experience, too-usual context switching is a sign of bad management. If things can't commonly flow from start to finish - something is not working. Unhealthy task switching will take place in departments that are confused about their business goals or in a department that is not prepared (from planning perspective) to handle support parallel to development.

Delays: Delays usually happen when we depend on other people or systems. For example, when a bug is discovered, a work item is created to describe it to the developer. If the work item does not describe the steps required to solve the bug with enough detail – the developer might waste time in solving it. The waste can come from steps that are hard to understand or from a developer who may get the entire project wrong and look for irrelevant solutions. Similarly, they may discover that the scenario is not even a bug – but a configuration issue or a feature. Other examples of delays might appear as dependencies on goods from one supplier; or a dependency on other teammates, etc. Delays are problematic because they disable the waiting resource Find your delays and resolve them.

Defects: Defects are a time bomb that cause exponential damages the more progress they make in the pipeline. A defect found in a small development iteration is easy to find. A defect that makes its way to production can have enormous economic implications. Quality is an important principle in Lean.

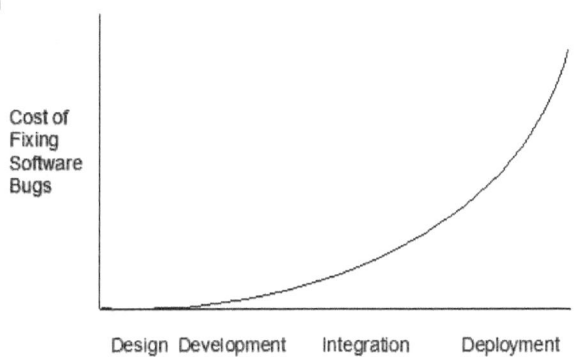

Cost of Fixing Software Bugs

Design Development Integration Deployment

[Source: https://buildsecurityin.us-cert.gov/articles/best-practices/security-testing/risk-based-and-functional-security-testing#refs]

Principle #2: Build Quality In

Lean distinguishes between two types of defect inspections: preventive and after-the-act. According to Lean methodology, the most important inspection is the preventive one. In software we use continuous integration and nightly builds to detect malfunctions as soon as possible. TDD and integration tests guard our progress. These are all preventive and proactive methods that maintain the quality of our code. Sometimes, NOT adding code is more important than adding it. Code that will never fail – is code that wasn't written in the first place. Tests guard the software system to enable team leaders to drive the team forward (and fast!).

There's a special and extreme tool called "stop-the-line" which is apparently essential to the success of the Lean approach. Any production line worker can stop the entire line when defects are detected, a malfunction occurs, or when anything that compromises quality is discovered.

Principle #3: Create Knowledge

You can't judge a man until you walk a mile in his shoes - and you can't understand the real design of a software system before you begin to implement it. Neither the architects nor the business owners and clients can predict the exact form of the system before it is created. This is one of the root causes of the waterfall model failure.

> Poppendieck: "Software development is a knowledge-creating process. While an overall architectural concept will be sketched out prior to coding, the validation of that architecture comes as the code is being written. In practice, the detailed design of software always occurs during coding, even if a detailed design document was written ahead of time. An early design cannot fully anticipate the complexity encountered during implementation, nor can it take into account the ongoing feedback that comes from actually building the software. Worse, early detailed designs are not amenable to feedback from stakeholders and customers. A development process focused on creating knowledge will expect the design to evolve during coding and will not waste time locking it down prematurely."

Principle #4 Defer Commitments

Here, Lean's recommendations are in exact opposition to Scrum: Lean drives us to defer our most important commitments to as late as possible. During Scrum iteration planning, a solution design is immediately suggested and decided upon during planning. Lean believes this approach to be problematic as it predicts a solution before it is validated in development.

> "One of the more useful goals of iterative development is to move from "analysis paralysis" to getting something concrete accomplished" (Poppendieck).

I remember once arguing with a developer and asking him to stop all development activity until he explained the exact design he would be following. I had expected him to provide me with a detailed design before development began. I was wrong. The system was very big and complex. Stopping work and forcing the developer to describe the solution with UML schemas or a presentation wasted time and was the wrong decision.

The Lean approach supports high level design with quantified, measurable criteria and requires expertise from the engineers in implementation of the design. In Lean, a system architect's job is to oversee the product with regard to customer ROI and make sure the team is providing excellent implementations that forge the complete product.

> "In preparing for battle I have always found that plans are useless, but planning is indispensable"
>
> -- Dwight Eisenhower

Principle #5: Deliver Fast

The beautiful concept of fast delivery is already well established in the Agile community. Scrum practitioners can easily relate to this in Lean methodology. The way to achieve this is to undertake the requirements and design processes as close to deployment as possible, so that no one will have the chance to regret decisions or be misunderstood in the process. In order to use this methodology, you must be able to break assignments into small incremental bits and implement a comprehensive automatic testing framework that is the safety net for all the changes.

I know a team that delivers to production multiple times a week(!). This eliminates so many limitations: There's no hardening period, for example. You just test the specific delivered feature and don't need to QA the entire system because you already know it's working. You're also protected by the testing framework that makes things much safer for you.

Delivering fast harnesses your client to the process. There must be someone on the other side who will be receiving all these quickly delivered goodies. This brings the client much closer to you, maintains flowing iterations and feedback, and ROI is expected to be much higher.

Just to be clear - this is not "quick and dirty". This is small incremental deliverables with a final outcome of a fully working maintainable product.

Principle #6: Respect People

Lean explicitly relies on the involvement and commitment of the people in the process.

If you want your team to "pull" work instead of "pushing" work items on them - you have to respect them and you have to delegate to them. There's no "one best way" to do things. There is always room for pluralism and discussion. The first chapter of this book deals with the development and nurturing of modern age employees and can help you achieve this.

The Poppendiecks marked three desired outcomes from the principle of respect:

1. **Entrepreneurial Leader** - The team leader described in this book fits this description. You handle your department like you would handle your own startup. Care about it, grow it, nurture it.
2. **Expert Technical Workforce** - The workforce should be expert in their domain. "Any company that expects to maintain a competitive advantage in a specific area must develop and nurture technical expertise in that area".
3. **Responsibility-Based Planning and Control** - The team should take ownership over their domain. An infrastructure should be set up in which team members pull work rather than having worked pushed upon them.

Principle #7: Optimize the Whole

Lean drives us to take responsibility over the entire value chain - not just responsibility for our comfort zone. Developers in a Scrum team can claim that they 'only do development' and not QA tests - but that approach doesn't contribute to the best achievable ROI. If a production problem occurs - a developer might be the best candidate to solve it and even create something to prevent future occurrences of the problem. A QA is not a developer - but if required to create an integration test with some coded logic - he or she should be able to do so.

The pipeline optimization is "from concept to cash" - not only an optimization of the development lifecycle. The chain starts from the people who sell a product to a client and ends with the people who might be integrating a system in a customer's site.

Lean is Surging

In many ways, Lean is better than Scrum, as it optimizes the whole chain. Scrum focuses on optimizing iterations. Lean naturally handles Macro affairs "from concept to cash". Lean breaks the problematic connection between planning and review. Lean's methodology allows us to adapt our deliverables to real world schedules. Lean allows us to seamlessly handle User Stories with bugs alongside any other work item type - and optimize our workforce to deliver everything as quickly as possible. Lean drives real cross-functionality in team and across teams. It is scalable, it has less managerial overhead, and most importantly, it is based on such a strong theoretical infrastructure that it is very hard to argue with its industry proven outcomes.

While Lean is more efficient than Scrum, Scrum does have some goodies that should be maintained in your work process. More on that further in this chapter.

Kanban

A few years after Scrum was so widely spread, cracks began showing in the system. Independent of each other, various teams found the time-boxed limitations a constraint. Miscalculated velocity caused overloaded sprints or otherwise sparse sprints. Deadlines were not adequately aligned with Sprint scheduling. Continuous bug fixing seasons did not match the Scrum meeting plan, especially because there is no planning involved and no user stories for bug fixing.

Teams began to ditch the Scrum fixed meetings schedule and began working on assignments in a flow. This is why Lean methodology is rising - and its main tool - the "Kanban" is rising along with it.

Kanban is very simple but it is very powerful. It is based on visualizing the work on a board that everyone can see and relate to. The team knows exactly what's going on by looking at the board - and further - the team is forced to invest effort on the real bottlenecks! Kanban is based on 3 simple pillars:

1. A visual board
2. Limits
3. Pull Work

The Visual Board

You can create whatever flow fits your needs. Let's take an example of a Kanban board:

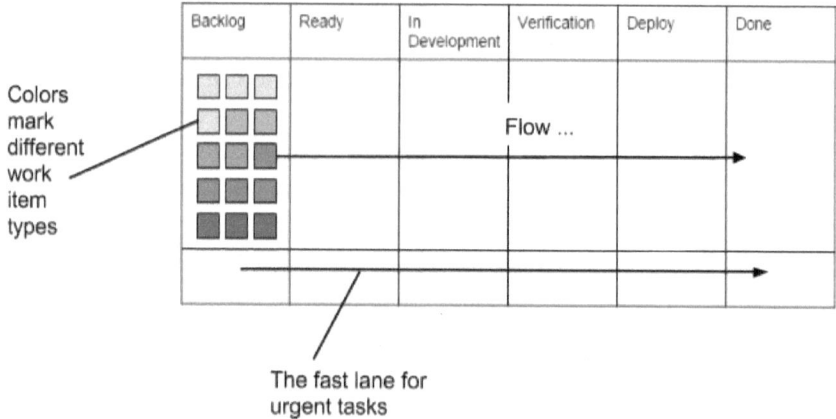

The fast lane for urgent tasks

Say we write down our User Stories on yellow sticky notes, our integration tests in green, maintenance in blue, etc. We prioritize tasks and put them all in the Backlog column. Sometimes this column is labeled "Workitem Backlog" or "WBL".

The Limits (WIP)

Kanban's beauty is that the board will SHOW you where your problems are because work items get STUCK in bottlenecks. Say for example you limit the board to have only 2 work items in each state (a.k.a. Work In Progress = WIP)

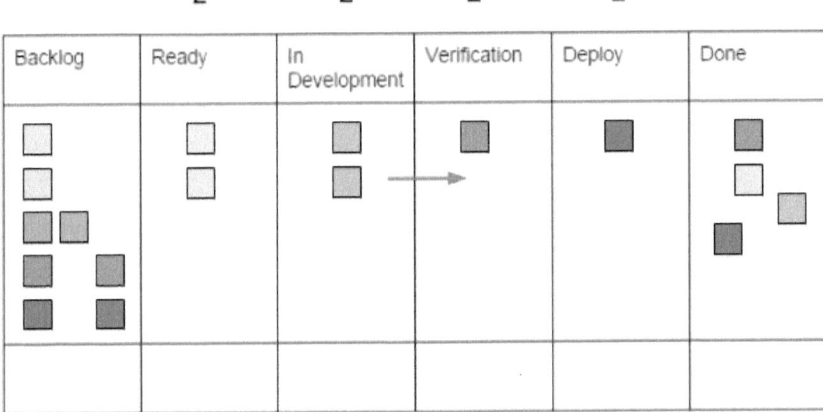

A team member comes to the board and sees what needs to be done next. They look at the work items and see that they cannot start a new task because the "In Development" segment is blocked. Instead, he or she will have to put effort into moving a work item from "In Development" to "Verification". They must somehow contribute to the development of one of the tasks, which will generally contribute to pushing the tasks towards completion.

With Kanban, a team can do "the right thing"; the thing that is required for effective flow. This is the difference between efficiency and effectiveness: "Efficiency is doing things right, while Effectiveness is doing the right things". This is what Kanban is all about - saving waste in the production line. Passing the most value to the customer instead of accumulating tasks in the pipeline.

Think of the cards on the board as inventory on a factory floor. Without limits, the fastest production lanes create inventory piles on the plant's floor.

Pull Work

The act of standing in front of the board and deciding what move to take is referred to as "Pull". Everyone on the team progresses assignments towards the exit on the right - downstream - pulling them from one state to the next. Opposite to "push" - we are aiming to create a "waste free" pipeline. If work is pushed in a rate faster than we can manage - the pipeline will be piled. Effort will be wasted on work items inside the pipeline instead of pulling work items towards the "Done" state.

Scrum and Kanban

Scrum and Kanban offer great insights that, when combined, give us a new way of managing software projects. Kanban does not force us to any organizational structure or any specific workflow. Kanban is elastic and can be adjusted according to need.

Scrum is a prescription for "managing software projects correctly" - and that is one of its highest values. It's something we can hold in our hands and feel confident about. Scrum's power in the industry is derived from the system being fixed and tangible. People need definitions. People need to KNOW they're doing things "right". They don't want to speculate.

What do YOU like about Scrum? I'll tell you what I like about it:

The roles are great (Scrum Master, Team, Product Owner). I love managing a cross functional team that can 'just do it' from design to deploy. I love working with a Product Owner who is enlightened, who can define requirements and definition-of-done and who shows the way to the client's highest ROI. I love being a team leader and Scrum Master - shepherding the activity towards accomplishing goals in harmony. I love that the Scrum Master facilitates the framework so people can feel confident within the boundaries set for them, so they may work together towards success.

Scrum meetings are awesome. Planning is extremely important. "Never start developing without planning" is an important insight. Review is critical: The team shows the Product Owner what was done, protecting us from delivering ineffective product that later will cost much more to fix. I love the retrospective meetings that streamline the entire process.

I want to keep the things that work for me, but I want to break the Scrum iterations. To me, iterations conflict with my real business needs to deliver content and handle production bugs. Maintenance issues never fit my Scrum cycles - and that always interrupts me. The fluent nature of Kanban works much better for me.

Scrum with Kanban is simple. Take the things you like about Scrum - and align them with the Kanban Flow.

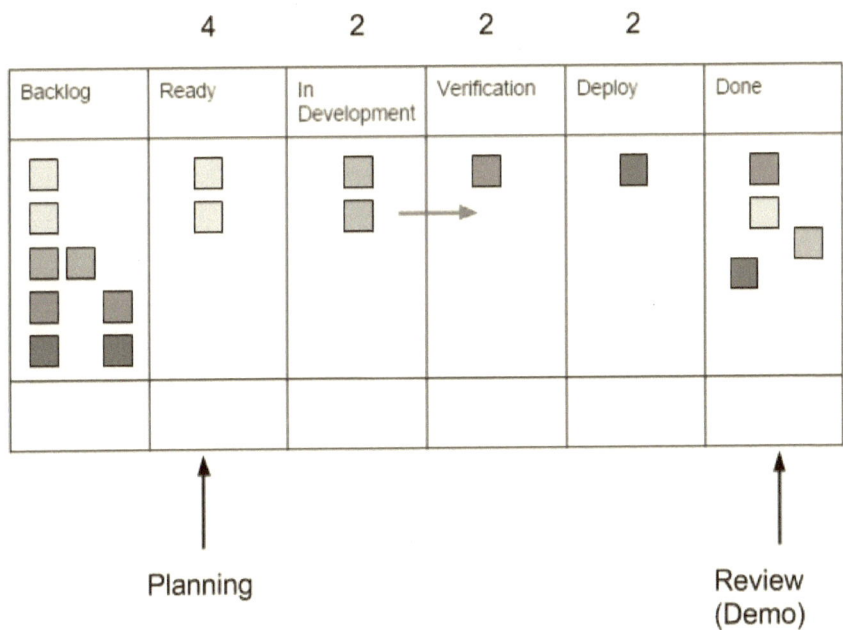

Now, you're free to execute a Planning meeting whenever the Ready state passes a predetermined threshold. For example, agree with your Product Owner that when there are only 2 items in the Ready state - a Planning meeting is called and more items will be added to Ready.

Now you're free to review and release whenever enough tasks are completed. You don't have to wait for synthetic iteration closure. Scrum with Kanban fits the mantra "Release early, release often. And listen to your customers".

Corey Ladas, a consultant in the field, authored a book and gave this combination a name: "Scrumban". Corey gave his interpretation to this idea back in 2009 (5 years ahead of this text). I first thought that

Scrumban was a whole different framework - but it is not. It's just your favorite Scrum parts spread on a Kanban pipeline. Corey provides a lot of great rationalization with in depth and historical analysis of "how we got here". It's a good read. In any case, Kanban is more fluent and efficient than Scrum in many real world software workshop contexts. It is simple to implement and simple to use. It is very intuitive and very efficient. It is easy to combine the best parts of Scrum with Kanban - and once you do this - a lot of Scrum limitations are solved automatically.

Part III

The Professional Team Leader

The Organization

It is important to understand your organizational structure. It is important to maintain good relationships with your colleagues, but it is also important to stand on your own when it comes to anything that affects your goal achievements. Winston Churchill once said: "You have enemies? Good. That means you've stood up for something, sometime in your life". Well, taking advice from a guy like Winston Churchill should be taken with extra precaution - but the principle of standing on your own is important.

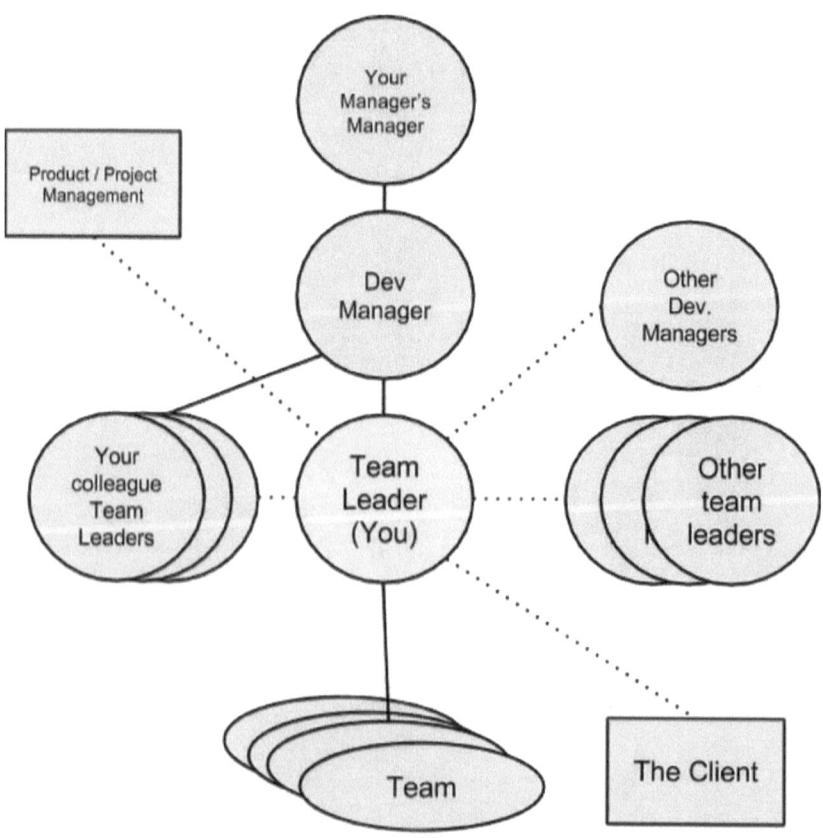

You, Your Manager and Your Team

This is your core group. We will go into depth about your manager and your team because they are the most important people with whom you are required to interact. Your team, as discussed in the first part of this book, is a kind of family; the practices of good parenting are in fact very similar to the practices of managing a team. Your manager, on the other hand, is a different story: Your manager is not your friend and certainly not a foe; although it may seem counterintuitive, you must manage your manager as well. We will review strategies for this below.

Colleague Team Leaders

These are your brothers and sisters. Just like in a real family - your relationship with these people can be complex. There can be jealousy - hidden or apparent. There might be a state of mutual accountability and friendly support. You and your colleague team leaders have one very big common interest - and that is your common manager.

You and your colleague team leaders will be the first to talk about problems you experience with your manager. To whom else would you turn? You don't go directly to HR because you'd probably want to solve your own problems first. You don't rush to your manager's manager because that would be too radical - especially for small issues.

Maintain good relationships with your colleague team leaders and always lend an ear or a shoulder when required. Remember that most of the time you're not required to DO something about what you're hearing - but rather just listen.

If you want to know what your team members think about you behind your back - a good idea would be to send your colleague team leaders to investigate. Feedback is important. Your employees may not be honest with you 100% of the time, especially if you're scary or doing a bad job. Some things are said indirectly so gather the information in creative ways.

Other Team Leaders

Other team leaders are those that are not directly managed by your manager. Other team leaders are your primary source of corporate gossip and promotional opportunity. They naturally understand your job dilemmas, your daily pressures, the spirit of your corporation and how everything affects you. You should consult with them on a regular basis. You can consult with them both on technical matters and managerial affairs. If there is a big managerial decision you need to take - they could be a good source of advice: they are close enough to understand your circumstances and considerations, but far enough to give you an objective point of view.

On the same note, other team leaders in your company can lead you to promotional opportunities that you may otherwise not find. They are in contact with other product managers and other development managers. If there is new opportunity in the company - outside your domain - they will hear about it before you do. You can get this information from them.

Other Development Managers

You need to be careful about these guys. They share the same managerial position as your manager. They don't owe you anything and they probably don't care about you. You should never complain to them about your manager. You can be friends with them - but don't open up to them because you don't know what they'll do with the information you give them. You might find your words travel through the organization and hurt you eventually. Just ask Benjamin Franklin - "Three [people] can keep a secret if two of them are dead".

Product Owner / Project Manager

In a technological based company there are two forces shaping the company's products: 'Technology Push' and 'Market Pull'. You are the technology pusher and the product manager is the market puller. Product managers translate the client's needs and desires into product features.

Modern theories of startup establishments talk about market pull as

THE ONLY consideration that shapes the product. They call this the Minimum Viable Product (MVP) which means you deliver the minimal set of features the client would want. MVPs represent the most value per dollar invested in development. MVPs are comprised of MVFs (Minimum Viable Features). Yet, the development group is NOT the one to set the priorities on what needs to be developed and delivered to the client.

Respect your product manager. Remember they represent the client - and the client is always right. Remember to always say YES to new demands. Provide assistance and support to the product manager. They might be technically clueless - so they would need the tech group to provide answers to questions they can't naturally answer.

You always need to display alternatives and call out considerations that are not obvious to the product manager. If a certain Customer Requirement (CR) has profound impact on the way your system works - it is your duty to call this out as an impediment to the CR at hand.

From Scrum methodology we learn that the product manager (a.k.a "Product Owner") must fully clarify their intentions before the beginning of the development cycle (this is the "planning" or "elaboration"). The Product Owner will also be the one to approve, at the completion of the development cycle, the final developed product (this is the Scrum "Review" or "Acceptance Test"). I believe that Product Owners should also regularly join the daily meetings - because one word from the Product Owner can save DAYS of developer work. They have the mandate to cut corners in the CRs - a mandate you do not have as team leader, once you committed to a certain development item.

I would like to suggest one very important practice: calling the Product Owner to the developers' computers before they check-in the code. This is a sort of pre-acceptance meeting. This meeting can be crucial sometimes because the Product Owner can comment on the development before it enters the Acceptance Test and QA cycles. This practice actually saves days of accumulated work for the team and for the company. Further, as time allows, having the Product

Owner around to consult with DURING development – can also be valuable. Don't surprise your Product Owner with the results of the development at the end of the iteration. Make him or her part of the flow.

Your manager will always receive feedback from the product manager about you. If you provide good support, you'll be praised. If you don't give good service, the product manager will complain about you. This is natural because the product manager and the development manager by definition work together.

The Client

In some cases, you will interface with the client. If earlier I advised to always say yes to the product managers, then, always always say yes to the client.

Be careful not to display internal team considerations or impediments to the client. The client doesn't care if one of your team members is on his annual vacation or that you have technical issues with your database in the lab. The client speaks in domain language and wants to hear answers in that language as well.

Don't commit to a client without consulting with your manager. In fact - you're not supposed to deal with the project schedule at all, as these tasks fall under the responsibility of the development manager and the product / project manager.

Sometimes the client is actually millions of users - not a specific person. In that case I would suggest you investigate the statistics from time to time. Try to understand usage patterns, how the product is used and why is it used the way it does.

Your Manager

As discussed above, your manager needs to be managed.

Understanding your manager's point of view is important. Managers want to know the bottom line - that everything is OK. Details are tedious and they make the managerial process more difficult. When a manager is too acquainted with the details, it usually means that at some point there was trouble that required their intervention. Development managers concentrate on strategic product road maps, on general HR planning, on training, on resources, and other higher-view aspects of management. The last thing a development manager is looking for is extra detail on a status of a single mission.

Setting Expectations

It is very important to have a conversation with your manager regarding his or her specific expectations from you. These are expectations that are different from the official corporate goals that they may share with you at a later time. For example: your manager might expect you to answer emails quickly, or may expect you to report progress at the end of each Tuesday. This book shows the fundamental goals a team leader should fulfil. You will find that your manager's specific expectations fit into these goals for the most part.

Ask your manager: "What would you define as 'successful' with regard to my team?" Ask your manager for HIS/HER goals as well. Ask them what you can do to assist them in achieving their goals. Ask directly for your manager's personal vision. How does he/she see the department a year from now? What is his/her strategy to get there? These are expectations that are not commonly shared between a development manager and a team leader until they "blow up" when a development manager is not getting what they expect. Make sure you send your manager a summary of this important conversation by email and make sure you have this conversation at least once a year.

Common Discussions

When talking to your manager - every word counts. Every intonation is interpreted. There's no small talk with your manager during work. There might be some small talk at lunch or after work hours - but not during work hours. Your discussions with your manager should be professionally measured.

All these suggestions are important because your manager expects to lean on your ability to control the team in a manner that makes the manager FEEL as though HE/SHE is controlling the team. Metaphorically speaking - when you give accurate and concise reports and when your team achieves its goals - your manager feels like s/he is hiking, leaning on robust and flexible walking sticks. When you give dim reports, act insecurely, question the status and don't control your people - your manager will feel as though s/he is hiking, leaning on ropes...

A common mistake is to engage in small talk on a mission that is in its intermediate state instead of its final state. Say you're working on something and agreed with your manager that you'll discuss the status at 12:00 PM. A developer comes by at 10:00 AM telling you that "he thinks he can solve everything in an hour". Suddenly you find your manager standing next to you on the way to coffee - asking you about the project status. Don't be tempted to report that "everything is well and that you'll have an answer in 1 hour". That's an ineffective practice for a number of reasons. First, developers are optimistic by nature - everything they estimate needs to be multiplied by a factor. But more importantly, since you can't really estimate the status of the assignment just because the developer said that "everything is ok" - there's no detail in this kind of report. The report doesn't include testing, integration, source control management, or any other detail that can just ruin your day. Tell your manager "my team in working on it. We'll discuss the status at 12:00 PM as agreed". Send the manager on his/her way - and gather all the details you need to complete the task professionally.

Status Discussions

Official status discussions are your opportunity to officially report the progress of an assignment. Usually these are fixed meetings agreed upon between you and your manager. When discussing the status - make sure to stick to the facts. Don't show confusion, don't make assumptions, and don't report according to gut feelings. The status is built from facts - not fiction. Be confident about what you know. Things you don't know - tell your manager that you'll 'check and report on it later'.

Delve into the code to be able to convey a clear confident message. Mark Zuckerberg's hacker approach is "code wins arguments". That is, in fact, your solution. No one can win an argument with you when you know exactly what the code does. When you see it with your own eyes - you are on top of the issue. You become familiar with the details, as you are required.

During status discussions, some managers might accuse you of not being familiar enough with the details. Don't try to justify yourself at this point because your manager obviously feels that s/he is not getting a clear picture from you in order to make decisions. Tell your manager that you'll investigate any detail that is not clear. Make it clear that you are on top of it. Then, schedule a consecutive meeting - and report the missing information.

Remember that status conversations are intended to give the manager a feeling of control - while also giving you the opportunity to use your manager's point of view to advise on solutions to problems.

Weekly Status

Every week or so, you should report the overall status to your manager. This is a one-on-one presentation to your manager. I really appreciate this practice because it is actually more important for the team leader than it is for the manager. The weekly status forces you to review everything you're doing. Almost every time I compose the weekly status, I get a cold reminder about tasks that I've neglected due to other important tasks that arose during the week.

The weekly report should be comprised of (almost) everything you're doing:

- The iteration plan or weekly schedule
- The actual capacity of your team
- The distribution of the team's effort on the work
- Discussion on impediments
- Discussion on special requirements
- Bug status
- Client status

- Human resources issues such as vacations and personal issues with the team
- Discussion of internal projects that you are doing or that you plan to do

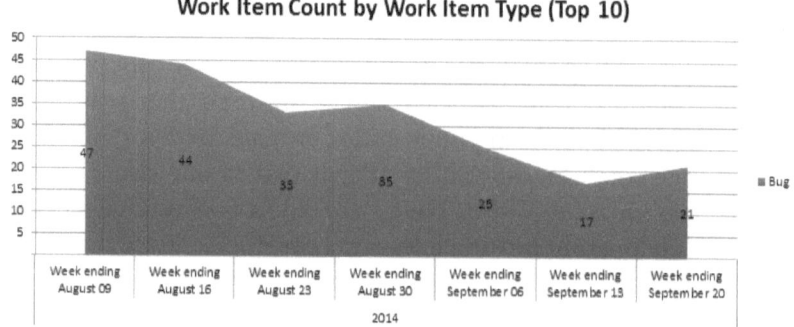

Example of a bug status slide

The idea of the weekly status meeting is to give your manager confidence that the processes in your team are working. Without the weekly status your manager will feel that s/he is in the dark and will use the only way they can to get the information: polling. Your manager will otherwise sporadically poll for the status which, in turn, will create a managerial overhead that you don't want.

Above I stated that your weekly status reports include almost everything you're doing. This is because you are not supposed to report anything besides facts. Facts, Facts, Facts. The weekly status is not the place to ponder or consult about future plans or general thoughts. That is for different discussions. The 'weekly' is a tactical report that smoothes frictions and lowers managerial overhead. Stick to the facts - and come prepared.

You may find that it is a burden to get some of the information for the weekly status every week. As a good manager you have a great tool: delegate. There are several advantages for delegating the tasks. First, your employees will be involved in the overall status and that gives them some way to get a little breathing space and see the big picture. The second advantage is obvious: you save time and practice your authority.

Your Territory

It is very important that you and your manager have an understanding of your responsibilities and your managerial territory. Define your mandate; agree on the processes you lead and what processes you don't lead. If your manager takes ownership on a mission - clarify to the manager that S/HE is the owner. It is the price they must pay for micromanagement if they choose to step into your shoes. If your manager prefers not to take ownership - clarify that there can only be one owner, either you or them. Boundaries are incredibly important.

> "Good fences make good neighbors"
> - Robert Frost

Taking ownership makes you a good manager. If you're independent in your domain it is evident that you're doing a good job. However, your manager may want to work directly with your people on a specific case. This should be a rare exception, as you are the manager of the team. People have one manager - not two. From a teammate's point of view it might be very stressful when your manager's manager comes in and gives orders. Additionally, your own managerial agenda might be different from your manager's agenda. It is very confusing for your team to suddenly take orders from someone else.

When your manager gets into your territory - it weakens you and your authority. Further - when your manager contradicts your decisions, especially in front of your employees, he or she reduces the meaning of your managerial role and harms the team's ability to rely on you and later function properly.

Production Issues

When working on live issues or problems that arise you should provide your manager with regular progress reports. Prepare these reports with your manager's point of view in mind. Your manager needs concise and clear reports that offer enough information to reflect the status, without an overflow of detail that can give them reason to worry. Lead your field of responsibility independently. If your manager pushes into your territory - push back and demand ownership of what's yours. For example, a good report would look as follows:

> "I am updating you that the client has encountered a production problem in connecting system A to system B. Andrey and Gabi from my team are on it. I will update you again in an hour."

When the problem is resolved - recap the status, first through a personal message and later with a summary email. A personal message would look like this:

> "Everything is now back to normal. The configuration in the tables was wrong after yesterday's version (wrong URL). I will send a recap email to everyone later tonight".

It is very important to transmit confidence, calmness, and professionalism with regard to production issues. You can throw in a joke or a sarcastic comment from time to time, as laughing a little in times of crisis is evidence of control and managing competence. Of course, don't make it a stand-up comedy show...

Principal Agreements

When making principal agreements such as major development decisions, career path decisions, product change decisions and the like - make sure the agreements are documented. Timelines should be interwoven with action items. State the attendees in the meetings in which agreements were made. Agreements' lifespan can be longer than office terms so you need documentation about what was agreed.

Capacity

It is part of your job to make sure your manager doesn't push your team to regularly work above its capacity. Since your manager doesn't have daily interaction with your team - the team may look like an inorganic resource that the manager can activate and deactivate at will. I will show you later exactly how to calculate the capacity so you can know what to demand from your manager and to what you can commit. Remember that a development manager who is constantly demanding work above capacity is a manager who will wear out your team and cause damage to your long term stability.

Taken from the book "The Living Company": "Companies die because their managers focus on the economic activity of producing goods and services and they forget that their organizations' true nature is that of a community of humans".

Commitments and Estimations

Specifically because of your successful background as a developer, you may be underestimating the time required for assignments. Your personal velocity might be faster than your team's velocity. Also, a development team is not only about development of code lines, but also about QA, versioning, graphics, User Stories, support - and a million other things that need to be considered when estimating an assignment. Sometime the development required is as simple as commenting a line of code - but the completion of the assignment may require days because of installation, QA, and integration issues.

The Development Team Leader Toolbox

Goals

Technology serves business needs. Team leaders are responsible for tactically leading the execution of the business plans. Beyond the iteration planning and daily goals – a team should be well connected to the business needs. As team leader you must be well informed, usually through your manager, about where you are leading your team. Ask your manager: "How do you see my team in 6 months?" "What would be considered success in 6 month for my team?" make sure you get straight, honest answers. Schedule a meeting with your manager regarding developments in your company. What are the expectations from your department? What are the expectations from your team?

As team leader you are measured by the following 6 goals:

1. On Time Delivery
2. Content
3. Quality
4. Interfaces
5. Team Spirit
6. Innovation

Achieving these goals is the key for a successful team. Before we discuss each goal individually – let's talk about goals in general.

Goals determine the agenda. Goals focus your team on tangible objectives and force you to work accordingly. Of course, there are both advantages and disadvantages to goal based planning and it's important to keep both those elements in mind. The main advantage of working according to goals is that it focuses the work force, overcoming people's natural tendency to scatter and miss what is actually expected of them. The main disadvantage of this type of work is that maintaining focus on goals makes you miss opportunities. Opportunities are, by their nature, short time framed and ad-hoc. When you're working according to goals you skip the interference – but you also skip the opportunities. It's not always possible to cash in on opportunities, but some managers will allow you to pursue them in one way or another. If the opportunities are too big for a quick-win, you might want to suggest that another group in your company have a look at it. If there's real value in it – someone may find it interesting enough to investigate. Your real focus in the corporation, though, should be meeting goals – not random opportunities.

In making decisions for your team, there are tradeoffs. Tradeoffs inevitably appear when we are limited by time or resources; in these situations, one thing will always come at the expense of the other. Referring back to your team's six goals mentioned above, look deeply at the list and you will find hidden contradictions. Your team, though, is required to successfully meet all goals. Take for example "On Time Delivery" vs. "Quality". It is obvious that when rushing things – developing 'quick & dirty' will help you achieve the On Time

Delivery. Quality will be sacrificed for the sake of schedule – but for how long can you keep this imbalanced approach? It is your responsibility as team leader to take all these elements into consideration and maintain a balance between the two.

Let's examine each goal.

<u>Goal #1: On Time Delivery</u>

Scheduling is related to setting-expectations. Your schedule affects everyone around you. Your clients, your managers, your colleagues and parallel teams. Planning is one of the most important tasks of your work.

Scrum teams work with iterations where each iteration is commonly 1-4 weeks in length. The 'X weeks' statement is the most dangerous assumption. For example: 2 weeks are 10 days – but do people really work 5 days per week? People are not machines. They take vacations, they get tired, they drink coffee, and they have personal issues and worries. Sometimes they just lack motivation. As team leader – you cannot plan for full 10 MD per developer per iteration. I use 9. Later I will show you how I calculate the 'rest-factor' of a developer. I calculate how much pressure a developer will feel at his work week.

Team leaders arise most commonly from a developer position, and developers are known to be optimistic by nature. Moreover – as team leader, you must have been the most gifted of your colleagues; that's what made you team leader in the first place. But your gift will be your curse when it comes to estimations. A common mistake taken by team leaders is to make estimations according to the time which they personally need to do an assignment – rather than the time it will take their employees to complete a task. As team leader you must be able to assess measure and adjust your team's capacity according to their capabilities rather than yours.

There are only specific cases where you'd give short estimations deliberately – and that is when you want to take an assignment that otherwise would not be given to you. If there is a new project in the company that you really desire – and other team leaders say it will take them 100MD to accomplish a POC – you can suggest taking the project and doing it in 80MD – thereby winning the race over the content. You take the risk of submitting the work behind schedule – but from my experience – when a team takes over a domain, it is very hard to take it away and give it to another team.

Goal #2: Content

A product's content is determined by 2 major forces: Technology-Push and Market-Pull. Market-Pull is where the marketing, sales or delivery body come to you and claim a feature that is interesting to your clients. The notion of Minimum Viable Product (MVP) uses the principle of Market-Pull as THE ONLY factor to determine your product's features. No one is really interested in the details of implementation – only the minimum set of requirements for a successful delivery.

Technology-Push on the other hand contradicts Market-Pull – and this, by definition, is your natural point of view.

Developers and team leaders are technology pushers. They want to stay on the cutting edge of technology. They are builders. They create. Although these human attributes are admirable, they tend to interfere with business. A team leader with a personal agenda is dangerous to the stability of the company. Team leaders who add in contents beyond the scope of the MVP and MVFs (Minimum Viable Features) are dangerous.

Everything you do should support the product-people's agenda. If you feel the product people are not requesting quality content or are not building the right thing, it is your job to offer them suggestions for improvement or quality solutions. You can show a competitor's system. You can give examples from internet sites and brochures. You can draw a sketch of your proposed solution, or you can create a POC. Be prepared to lose most of these confrontations.

Goal #3: Quality

Measuring and production of quality software is a central theme in the industry. The overall outcome of the team's work should be of high quality, and that's why the team leader should be very acquainted with how quality can be measured and achieved. Although this book does not deal with the subject of quality, Appendix A contains my recommendations for the must-reads industry cornerstone publications on this topic. The discussion on quality is vast and deep, and should be taken very seriously by the team leader. You should know what to demand of the team and teach the team to demand quality of themselves. Achieving working software can be done in so many different ways, but there are long and short term implications for how things are getting done. Bad quality harms the product, but also harms the team motivation because developers don't want to handle ugly legacy software. They feel bad when they have to twist their own arms when maintaining bad quality software. In general, good quality is a desired state, and the team leader's job is to achieve and maintain that state.

Goal #4: Interfaces

Your overall success as a team leader is dependent on your relationship with your peers, colleagues and clients. Earlier, we discussed these relationships in detail. Maintaining regular and open lines of communication with all the different interfaces as is appropriate to your role will make a huge difference to your team's goals and your success in your job.

Goal #5: Team Spirit

Your team's team spirit depends primarily on you. In order to achieve powerful team spirit in your employees, remember the key is to create a work environment where each of your employees can feel that they achieve full peace of mind. When people are troubled or feel threatened - they won't be effective and the team will not function as it should. Remember the 3 Adlerian pillars: people need to feel they belong, necessary, and capable.

Innovation is the icing on the cake. If you succeed to pull an innovative effort from your team - it is a strong indication that you're on top of the game. In some cases you will find that you're drawn to developing dedicated tools for your team's needs. This is a good place to start implementing innovation. You know the details of your domain and detail spawns creativity.

Planning the Day

A lifehacker's quote on planning the day:

> "He who every morning plans the transaction of the day and follows out that plan, carries a thread that will guide him through the maze of the most busy life. But where no plan is laid, where the disposal of time is surrendered merely to the chance of incidence, chaos will soon reign."

Victor Hugo

Planning is proactive. It is never a passive act. Practically, I (almost) always start my day with setting my own daily goals. As team leader - I may also write down my expectation from each of my team members.

Your Personal Plan

For myself, I use a notepad++ txt file that is always opened on my desktop. I have about 4000 lines after a year on a job. It contains everything I do and think during the day. It looks like this-

Today
----
1. Has John's env resolved ?
2. Review client's bugs
3. Fill form 119
4. Work with Anthony on the model
5. Alicia should see the proper service with data
6. Understand Pavel's input

7. Print functionality problem
8. Gabi and Andrey - improve workflow
9. Make sure with David that they are taking the correct branch

Although you have a plan for yourself - remember that your efforts should be mostly focused on releasing impediments for your team. You are mostly a Servant Leader, and that means you have to service your team members, manager, product owner, and everyone else. If you do want to complete something extremely important that can be done just by you - I recommend taking a side room and disappearing for an hour or two. Complete your critical tasks and go back to your seat as fast as possible.

Remember you're a team leader. You can't disappear for too long. People rely on you.

Generally, you work according to priority. In theory, you only do the high priorities and never the lower priorities. But what if someone in the company asks you for a favor or for a quick answer about something?

It is said that when developers context-switch, it generates waste. But context switching is a necessary reality for a team leader. Frankly, it is a matter of decision to make context switching feasible for you. If you decide that you are willing and able to help and context switch - you will succeed. If you have decided in your mind that context switching bothers you, then you are destined to fail at the attempt. Remember that the team leader doesn't have the privilege to shut himself off and work solely on an assignment as does a developer. You have to be responsive to your environment. On the same note, if you are required to perform a long task that requires concentration and you did not retire to a side room - do ask the people addressing you to schedule a meeting for later - or to come back at a later time. In some cases, if you're lucky enough, people will find a way to help themselves.

When someone indeed asks you for something you can never say "I'm sorry, there's no time". There isn't such a thing as "no time" - there is only priority and laziness. Even if an assignment is of lower priority for you - it doesn't mean that it is never to be done. It should be done at a later time - after the high priorities are complete. Don't regard this as a favor, but as an integral part of your responsibility of making everything tick. Your peers have their own goals and priorities, which may be different than your own. You are expected, however, to serve and collaborate so your peers won't get stuck on their flow. If work items that are not prioritized seem to be taking over your schedule – you may involve your manager and ask to review the priorities. You might have the wrong picture on the overall plan.

Team Plan

In order for my team to focus on their goals on the first day of the week, I sit at the end of the weekend and prepare a summary of expectations for the coming week. Before I conclude my list, I discuss it on the phone with my manager. Discussion with the manager is healthy because the manager almost always has a different view of priorities than you.

Here's a sample of an email I send my team before the week begins:

Team,
These last 2 weeks we discussed our goals of stabilizing the system in order to enhance the reliability of our product. This approach will lead us to the next business goals and I'm confident we can deliver and make our solution echo in the company.

This week we'll continue our efforts with the following highlights:
- Gabi – Release of version 5.0.6
- David – Start User Stories and fixes for next release
- Andrew – Enhance performance on module X
- Alicia – Module 1 and module 2 bug fixes
- Dana – Bug fix #154879 and continue Integration Tests

When there's too much to do

> "Begin at the beginning," the King said, very gravely, "and go on till you come to the end: then stop."

- Lewis Carroll, Alice in Wonderland

Daily goals

Agile and Lean methodologies are advocates of setting timely goals with emphasis on personal and team commitments. A team member will commit to an amount of work according to his or her own estimation. Daily goals are an important and effective practice. Remember -

"Work expands to fill the time available for its completion"

-- Cyril Northcote Parkinson (Parkinson's law)

Uncontrolled Daily Goals

Sometime it is ok to just let go of your team member's schedule. People can't live under constant pressure. Commitments are effective but they are also very stressful. Not everyone is built for pressure and surely creativity does not commonly occur in the presence of constant stress. Your team shouldn't always work at full capacity all the time.

Bi-Weekly Personal Meetings

Communicating with your team members is important. I recommend you schedule a bi-weekly meeting (once every two weeks) with each of your team members. If it is too much - do it once every month. In my country it is common to also discuss a bit of personal affairs during this meeting. In other countries - that practice is practically illegal.

Some team leaders may be hesitant to introduce a personal conversation. It is natural to be hesitant to undertake this type of talk. It will help if you prepare yourself for the conversation. Write down an agenda. You can talk generally about your profession, about technological advances, or discuss a nice story you heard in the company. This conversation is the time to ask about the employee's feelings regarding certain events in the company: "how do you feel about the changes in sales department?" you can ask for feedback about your own actions as manager.

Code Review

Code review is an important tool that must not be neglected even if you think there's no time to undertake it. Code review lets you understand what is REALLY being done. The real complexity of software cannot be captured by verbal explanations - only by reading lines of code. Code review shows you how things are done - if things were developed as planned or whether corners were cut to achieve a goal. It reveals the real practices and conventions.

Code review is the best way to connect you, as team leader, to the nuts and bolts of the implementation. It gives you the ability to later answer in detail to your manager, the product owner, and any other organizational interface.

Managing is very much about measurement: the rule is that you cannot manage what you cannot measure. Code review is a measurement of quality.

Developers who know their code will be reviewed tend to do a better job because they know that there's someone looking above their shoulder. They ponder more about the practices and they take extra steps to avoid known conflicts with the code reviewer.

Code review should not only be undertaken by the team leader. It's an excellent practice for developers to code review each other. It promotes communication between team members and aligns the practices in the team. Beware though of rivalry between two teammates. If you have such a relationship in a team, its preferable not to assign them to code review each other because it may end up in a fight.

Code review is sometimes misinterpreted as criticism and central management. While I can relate to this point of view, make it clear to the team that this practice benefits everyone. Explain to your team what YOU are gaining from the process. Make sure they understand that you are doing code review to learn - not criticize. Explain that code review is a good opportunity for a fruitful discussion, which will be much better than any other time in the team. Explain the value of conventions and that your code review is indeed a tool to align everyone on the team to follow these conventions. Talk about code review in the daily meeting to remind everyone how important it is and why it is being done.

There are times when you have your hands so full that you cannot address a code review session. If you don't want to hold back the development cycle until you are available to conduct a code review - do it retrospectively. You can do this by going to your code management system, clicking history, and investigating the developers' check-ins. Code that was checked in, but you don't really know how it works - is code that you can't really trust. You see it working, but you don't know how. You might be looking at bad practices under a pretty cover. This kind of thing tends to blow up in the long run.

Brainstorming

The beauty in a diverse team is the plurality of viewpoints. Different people think differently and people build upon other's ideas. This is brainstorming. When I begin a new development - I will probably consult with my team about the solution. I create a special meeting to review a design or to think together about possible solutions to problems.

I personally don't believe in large forums as a venue for brainstorming. In large forums there is more noise than actual thinking - and it is hard to express really deep good ideas. A group of 2-3 relevant people, including you, is enough in most cases for an effective brainstorming session. While some claim that having everyone involved at the outset gets everyone committed, simplifying the execution, I believe that if a team operates well, they communicate with each other all the time and there's no real value in wasting everyone's time for brainstorming. Brainstorming is construction of deep thought ideas that need focus and intimacy.

Planning the capacity

Your team members can be thought of as resources with a certain capacity. In Scrum the capacity is planned in chunks of 1-4 weeks. Theoretically, each teammate has 10 working days (WD) within the 2 weeks chunk - but it is good practice to plan the capacity for 9 days per 2 weeks because of the human factor e.g. eating, small talk, getting tired etc. In fluent frameworks such as Lean, planning the general capacity for the next 2 weeks is just as useful as in Scrum iterations.

Planning should consider everything that might (and will) take place during work. Basically, Tasks are built from functional requirements and QA periods - but they also include satellite issues such as security, performance, refactoring, and the like. People's capacity changes and is influenced by a wide range of reasons, from motivational changes and vacations to planned and unplanned maintenance. Time is also spent on versioning, tools, blocking requirements, and more.

So how do we plan? We use a simple chart to give us an overview of resources per project. Take for example a team of 4 developers and one QA. The team works for 3 clients, while also developing some internal projects.

Let's examine 2 iteration plans:

Overall Capacity

	Dev 1	Dev 2	Dev 3	Dev 4	QA	Comments
Iteration #1 (Sep 7)	9	9	8 (day off)	4 (on client site)	9	
Iteration #2 (Sep 21)	9	9	9	9	9	Release version 5.0.6

Iteration capacity #1

Sep 7	Dev 1	Dev 2	Dev 3	Dev 4	QA	Total
Project 1	5				2	7
Project 2		9			2	11
Project 3	4				3	7
Project 4			9		2	11
Total	9	9	9	4	9	40
Stress Ratio	1	1	1.125	1	1	1.025

Iteration capacity #2

Sep 21	Dev 1	Dev 2	Dev 3	Dev 4	QA	Total
Project 1	9				2	11
Project 2		9				9
Project 3	2				5	7
Project 4			9		2	11
Total	11	9	9	8	9	44
Stress Ratio	1.22	1	1	0.88	1	1.022

The first table is the overall capacity plan. What we're seeing is that on the September 7th iteration, developer #1 will have 9 WD whereas developer #4 is planned to be on the client site and will have only 4 days to develop. On the September 21st iteration (two weeks after September 7) everybody is in the office - so they have 9 WD each.

In the iteration capacity plan - we can see a general distribution of the work days per developer per project. Sometimes - the planned work is less than the capacity of the developer, and sometimes there is pressure so the required capacity is greater than the developer's capacity. For example, you can see that in the September 7th iteration, developer 3 will have to do his 9 WD commitment - even though he is taking a day off.

You might assume that working **above the capacity** or **below the capacity** will have consequences. Take a look at the calculated Stress

Ratio. It is the division of the planned capacity with the actual capacity. When I discovered the Stress Ratio I realized that I can quantify and plan my team's mood and motivation. When you work your team above the capacity for a long time - you wear out your team. When you work your team below the capacity for a long time - you make them indifferent.

You must have a clear plan before the iteration begins, and you must share this plan with your team so everybody knows what they are facing.

The required capacity will be determined according to your favorite Agile methodology. You will sum up the prioritized tasks, quantify them into working days, normalize them according to each developer's velocity - and assign them into the iteration plan.

Efficient Meetings

Meetings take a significant amount of your schedule as a manager thus meetings should be understood. Meetings have a purpose - they align collaborators with ideas and most importantly they produce action items. Plan or action items are contents with a schedule and assigned resources. For example, in a morning meeting with your manager you agreed to investigate an urgent issue with 2 developers and discuss the results of that investigation again at 14:00 at your manager's office.

> Content = the investigation
> Resources = 2 developers + team leader
> Schedule = 2 hours

Meetings must be strictly managed. They should have a defined agenda that is transmitted to participants so that they may each prepare for the meeting and contribute. Keep the meeting to the allocated time frame. If a meeting is scheduled for an hour but there are no conclusions or action items when the time is up, close the meeting and schedule another at a later time. Often, the reason no conclusion was reached is that there was missing knowledge or data for a fruitful discussion. Sometimes, participants need to prepare better and think of alternatives to suggested problems. In my experience, it is better to stop at the allotted time and start again with fresh perspective. I have seen that too often, meetings that go far over the allotted time tend not to be productive.

There's a Hebrew expression that states, "A shy person doesn't learn, a severe one doesn't teach." Don't be afraid to ask questions, and be responsive and generous when you are asked questions. If something is unclear - just ask. Ask once, ask twice - make sure you understand the material. If a sub group of attendees takes the conversation to topics with which you are unfamiliar, tell them that their 'private discussion' is not clear and if not appropriate to elaborate in this meeting, perhaps the conversation over the unclear matter should be taken to another meeting. This is especially relevant to your first period in a new job where the domain of the business is commonly unclear. Always request that any unclear information be clarified on the spot.

Following certain meetings, it is very important to send the minutes to all attendees because actions are derived from the principal agreements in the meeting. For example, you might find yourself working on issues that were agreed upon in the meeting, but that later the other parties will not recall or remember differently. Discussions about career paths and the like must be documented in writing because managers are replaced and office terms end - while agreements last beyond these periods of time.

I have learned that more often than not, people in corporations tend to speak about almost everything that comes to mind in meetings. Some people think that these are social events,
'get-togethers" of some sort. Some employees, it seems, think that meetings are a good place to stand out from the crowd and show how smart they are. This kind of behavior is annoying and unconstructive to the company. For myself, I have developed the practice to mostly listen to my colleagues during meetings. I speak concisely on the discussed issue only and always make sure attendees leave with action items.

Speak short and concisely - and every word you say will scorch the conversation like lightning. Speak like a sprinkler - and no one will take your words seriously enough.

In the software industry discussions often deal with the matter of the code itself, with logic, or with a system's way of working. An "if-else" or A-"Send-To-B" discussion if you will. Therefore, we can leverage our best practice tools of communication in the form of diagrams. For example, you can use UML diagrams in the form of sequence diagrams, state machine diagrams or Use Case diagrams. You can also select to present flowchart diagrams. Anything is better than just verbally mumbling over a feature with hand waving gestures.

Let's examine some of the most useful diagrams:

Sequence Diagram

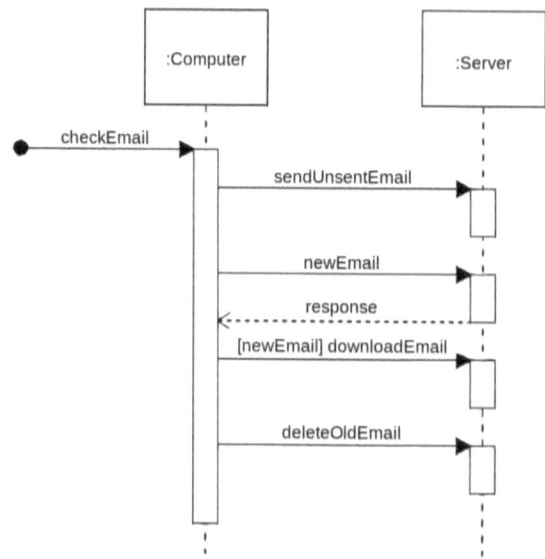

"A sequence diagram is an interaction diagram that shows how processes operate with one another and in what order... It depicts the objects and classes involved in the scenario and the sequence of messages exchanged between the objects needed to carry out the functionality of the scenario. Sequence diagrams are typically associated with use case realizations in the Logical View of the system under development. " [Wikipedia]

Use Case Diagram

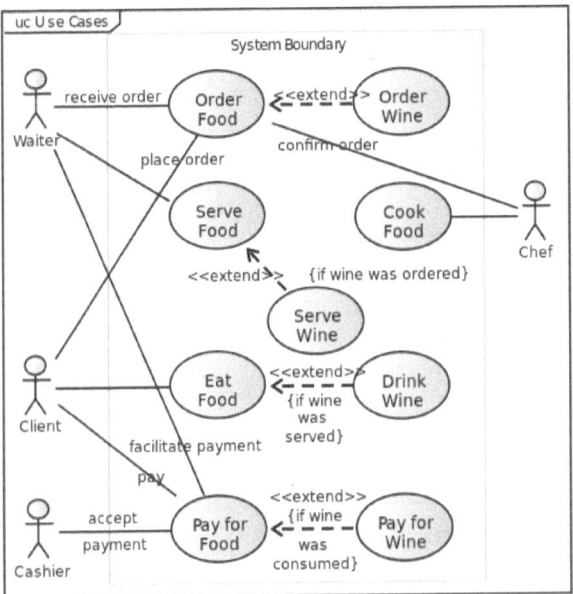

"A use case diagram at its simplest is a representation of a user's interaction with the system and depicting the specifications of a use case. A use case diagram can portray the different types of users of a system and the various ways that they interact with the system. This type of diagram is typically used in conjunction with the textual use case and will often be accompanied by other types of diagrams as well." [Wikipedia]

Flowchart Diagram

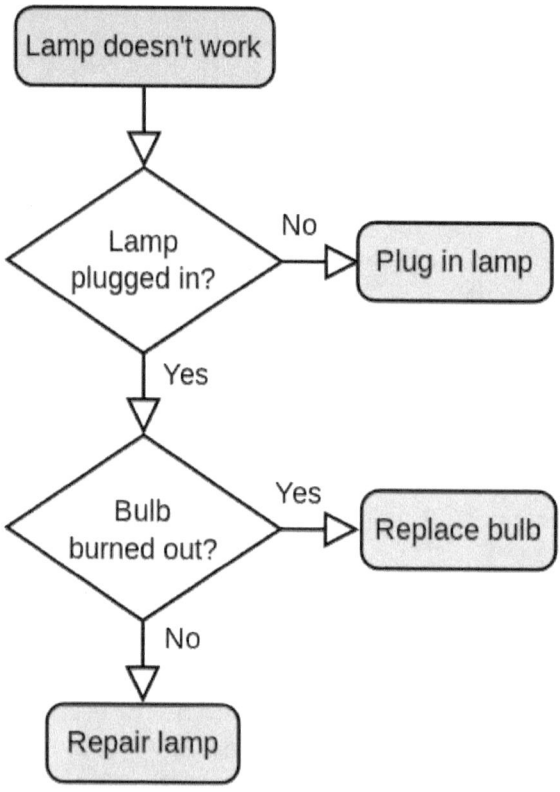

"A flowchart is a type of diagram that represents an algorithm, workflow or process, showing the steps as boxes of various kinds, and their order by connecting them with arrows. This diagrammatic representation illustrates a solution model to a given problem. Flowcharts are used in analyzing, designing, documenting or managing a process or program in various fields." [Wikipedia]

The above charts are what I personally found myself commonly using, however every domain and business will find the appropriate charts to express their ideas. Take the time to examine the best practice charts. Search for "UML diagrams" on google. Take the time to prepare for meetings with these diagrams so you can lead the conversation constructively and maintain the thread of thought.

Planning the Code

People like Agile development because it saves the headache of working with large designs. Working with Agile feels like you were granted authority to "run-wild" and "just do" the things that need to be done to accomplish the business goals.

As team leader, you must ask for the more detailed plan - even if it only exists in the developer's head. When a developer announces that he's going to do something in the system, ask: "How are you going to achieve that?" Following the answer, refine your questions further: "Are you sure the assumptions in your solution are true?", for example. Ask for alternatives: "Is there another way to accomplish this?" Try to understand if there are faster ways, smarter ways, and cheaper ways - to accomplish the action item that is being discussed. Write down the steps your teammate suggests. This will help you follow up on the process later on.

After the plan is detailed - ask for estimations in terms of time and risk. Often, as a result of the analysis, you will be able to set milestones that can be checked and discussed with the teammate. Detailed tasks make the process manageable. It is better than simply 'throwing' the developer in the water and asking him to achieve his or her goal.

When and if you're not getting straight and clear answers, it is probably because the teammate him/herself does not understand the details. As a rule of thumb - if one cannot explain in simple terms what they're doing - then they don't really understand what they're doing. Send your teammate to investigate further and redo the plan, asking the same initial questions as above.

Retrospective

In order to create a healthy work framework, you need a method of feedback. Retrospective meetings are feedback meetings and highly important to calibrate your team's process. Feedback is more than a slogan. It is a rule of nature. Every system in nature has a feedback loop and thus our management systems must contain feedback loops as well.

In a retrospective meeting every team member will express their impressions of the work being done. Ask each teammate to prepare for the meeting. Your manager and the product owner should participate in the meeting as well. Here's a sample calendar event for you to send to your team:

> Team,
> At the end of the iteration we'll conduct a retrospective discussion.
> In this meeting we'll discuss lessons learned.
> Please prepare your notes as follows:
> - 2 issues to maintain
> - 2 issues to improve
>
> Thanks

Start the meeting by presenting your own insights. Let everyone express themselves including your manager and the product owner. Allow discussion, but don't let one individual take over the discussion. Make sure the participants are talking to each other rather than reporting to you.

Retrospectives are an opportunity to complement and encourage people on their performance. Remember! There is a difference between encouragement and praise! On matters which need improvement, NEVER blame. The team has joint responsibility - and the team leader has overall responsibility. If the QA, for example, complains that he didn't have time to check the version thoroughly, it's not exclusively his fault. Maybe the team leader didn't plan ahead. Maybe the developers had too many unplanned reopened issues. There are tons of reasons why things go wrong. A retrospective is NOT an opportunity to crucify people - but an opportunity for discussion and improvement.

The frequency of retrospective meetings depends on the stability of your team's process. Stable teams have come to a steady state and "work smoothly" so they usually require fewer retrospective meetings. Young or otherwise less stable teams would require more feedback to get to a steady state and thus require more retrospective meetings.

Documentation, Education and Recruitment

The software industry is the knowledge industry. Knowledge and skill are what makes work possible in your team. You must take on a constant mission of creating documentation, presentations, tutorials, and any other educational content and tools.

Educational tools enable fast transfer of knowledge between existing team members and fast transfer to new members once they join. Your ability to absorb turn over in your team is derived from your ability to quickly train new employees. Another advantage of being proactive in education is that it dismantles unacceptable phenomena such as employees leveraging some unique knowledge for job security. Power centers of this form are bad for everyone.

Documentation in this sense is not 'code documentation' - but rather documentation that addresses major functionalities that support the business. You can also document significant events that occurred in your team such as stories about an evolutionary version, stories about unique collaboration, stories that reflect customer behavior, and so forth.

Personally, in my company, I also created presentations on domains that don't belong to my team in order to educate the team members on processes that happen beyond the scope of our team. I believe in broad vision as a tool for better decision making so I found it important to give my team these types of contents as well.

Systems & Diagnostics

Giving your team excellent infrastructure resources is a very important part of your job, as system environments are an important part of the work flow. They are the playgrounds on which the team plays. Friction arises when resources are sparse or misallocated. You have a responsibility to provide fast and reliable environments and allow the team to run freely upon them.

The required environments mostly follow the below paradigm –

Production Environment

This is the holy temple where the code eventually does its magic. You should be able to provide the team comprehensive tools to diagnose production problems if and when they occur.

Staging Environment

Just before the code goes to production - it is installed in an environment that simulates production almost identically. Sometimes staging connects directly to production data sources. The staging environment is the step before production.

QA Production Environment

The QA Production contains the environment closest possible to the production environment. QA Production is used as an environment to reproduce production problems when they occur. Without this environment you can get caught with your pants down when things go wrong in production because you will not be able to quickly reproduce production problems anywhere but here.

QA Latest Environment

The QA Latest environment is used for tests on the coming releases. This QA environment should be sterile from developers' intervention. The QA conducts their tests here to verify that the code is of sufficient quality. Don't underestimate the QA's demand to keep the environment sterile. Developers will contaminate it to save time for themselves because they don't want to "waste" time on installing environments - only on code. Don't let them touch it.

Development Environment

A development environment can be a developer's computer or other computers that contains the latest code. The developers can do anything that comes to their minds on those systems without fear of ruining anything in the work flow.

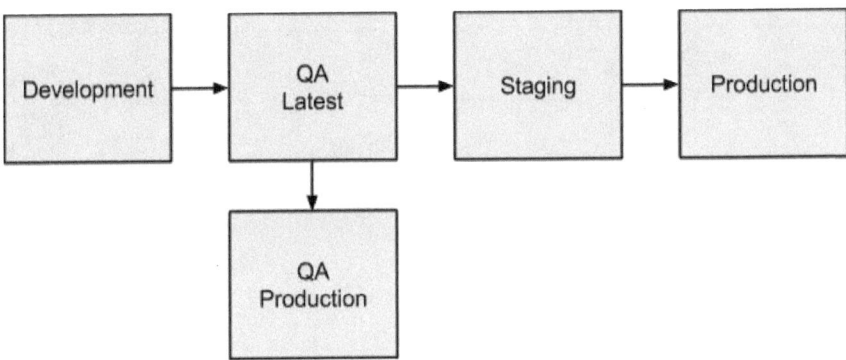

When things go wrong, make sure you are trained and equipped to handle production issues. Don't wait for bad days to discover that you don't know how to monitor and analyze your systems. You need eyes and ears in production. For example, working on Microsoft server environments would require you to control the following tools:

1. Perfmon
2. SQL Profiler
3. System Logs
4. Use the System Monitor
5. Possibly Wireshark® or Fiddler®
6. Read the event viewer
7. IIS Diagnostics
8. Etc.

Remember to prepare ahead with logs, simulators, or any other data source from which you can gather information (that are specific to your systems) in order to analyze production issues. If you need communications to remote sites - test that they are working at least once a week. Do anything that you can to prepare for production problems so you don't get caught by surprise.

Epilogue

In this book we reviewed three aspect of the team leader's job: First and foremost is the Adlerian framework that provides the toolset required to motivate and maintain a productive team. Second, the Agile and Lean workflows that give us the schedule framework required to develop and maintain software products. Third, we reviewed professional management tools required to operate the day to day work with peers, management, goal achievement and more.

We reviewed the central Team Leader Dilemma – to develop or to manage. Team leaders can't really do both at the same time and you need to be very aware of the influences that each mode has on a team.

The team leader's job is a complex assignment and is not to be taken lightly. It is not merely the responsibilities of a good developer promoted to manager. It is a very special position which combines business, technical and HR responsibilities. The job demands your development of both EQ and IQ. Team leaders are required to produce high quality products, while maintaining highly motivated teams; they are required to remember code lines and system behavior while listening to the team's whisperings of the heart.

The team leader's job is very demanding, but it is also very rewarding. It's a significant and challenging role that affects both the business and the team members' lives. If all team leaders would be "Adlerian" and provide for the team members' emotional needs, our collective work would be more enjoyable and the industry's creativity and productivity will rise.

Thank you for reading The Adlerian Team Leader. I hope the book helps make a better industry, which is empathic, constructive and fun!

Good Luck!
Or Berkovitch

Join our blog at **Adlerian.org** for further discussion and information on the Adlerian approach and the Team Leader's job.

Appendix A: Software Quality

The Mythical Man-Month

Fred Brooks's book "The Mythical Man-Month: Essays on Software Engineering". Most of the book shockingly stands the test of time. It discusses and hypotheses on the structure of software teams. Brook's reveals the developers inner thoughts and feelings mapping the joys and woes of the craft, thereby binding the developers feeling with the success of the software project. The matter of emotion will be addressed years later by the Agile programming movement. The book emphasized the importance of communication between team members and unconsciously seeks to break out of the waterfall methodology in software development. The book also suggests a term called "No Silver Bullet" that claimed that "a decade would not see any programming technique that would by itself bring an order-of-magnitude improvement in software productivity". While the industry still suffers from bad success ratio of large software projects - there are now several "Silver Bullets" such as source code management systems (TFS / Git / Mercurial), smart step-by-step debugger, code analysis tools, Agile methodologies, cloud infrastructures, and more. Despite all these advances, we still can't say that there is ONE best way to create code - and that is absolutely fascinating!

Design Patterns

In object oriented programming, Design Patterns is the collective best-practice of the software industry. A design pattern describes the structure you would commonly implement to achieve software functionality.

The original book introduces a basic list of design patterns. The industry has further enhanced and perfected the list with special attention on IoC methodologies that comprise a multiplicity of design patterns all wrapped into one.

It is common that questions about design pattern are asked in job interviews. An ineffective question would be the simple one: "What design patterns do you know?" Design patterns are contextual by nature and therefore the question needs context. So when you interview try asking a good question like "How would you implement..., etc. " good professionals will know to incorporate the design pattern in their answers.

Knowledge of design patterns is also important because when we refactor our code, we in fact restructure it towards the design patterns. If we don't know what we're aiming towards when refactoring - we're just messing around with the code.

Refactoring

"Refactoring is a disciplined technique for restructuring an existing body of code, altering its internal structure without changing its external behavior." (Martin Fawler).

The skill of refactoring stands above many of the skills required to become a good developer and team leader. I cannot emphasize the importance of this skill enough. Developers under code review should witness their team leader refactor the code from time to time and therefore this is a critical skill for team leaders.

Gloves off...

Refactoring is hard in practice because of 2 irrelevant reasons: it takes courage and it requires a mandate. Managers don't like to change things because of the business risks. Developers are afraid to change anything because of their limited mandate.

Refactoring is a game changer - but since it is a concept that does not exist in any other engineering practice besides software development, it makes it hard to rationalize to management. Management may claim: "But it worked before", "I am sure the company that built this for us knew what they were doing", "Just plug this in there and it will work".

Refactoring is at the heart of any modern software development methodology. If it is not embraced by management, it may be a sign that the company has no real expertise in software development; it's a real sign that any code development should be outsourced to external third parties. Refactoring is tied to long-term goals. If a development group is forced to hot-fix all the time and is not allowed formally to refactor as a methodology - it is a symptom of a sick stressful culture or of a company without a future.

To be honest, I myself haven't found a powerful way to explain why it is so important and why developers should spend so much time and effort refactoring instead of throwing in more functionality. I do know this: if you do not have your management's back regarding this, include it as a part of your tasks - and just do what you need to do to get the job done. Be confident in your skill and knowledge and work towards creating a full coverage of integration tests to keep you safe from harm.

Domain Driven Design

Domain Driven Design (DDD) is a cornerstone book on systems design. When I refactor a system, when I build anything - I always think in DDD terms.

The author, Eric Evans, made a huge contribution by laying out the bridge between requirements and implementation.

I believe that Evans has given us the closest thing to a "Silver Bullet" in the form of fundamental building blocks of a software construct: The Layered Architecture, Entities, Associations, Value Objects, Services, Modules, Aggregates, Factories, and Repositories.

The approach of the anemic model vs. the rich model is not discussed in the book, which I think is an important conversation. DDD might give you the impression that you can implement all your logic in the Services layer - but that is not the case.

After taking so much pleasure from the first part of the book, readers forget to continue reading the second part where Evans covers the DDD approach in enterprise systems. Designing bounded domains that work together, while keeping their borders well defined will help teams work together in large scale. I've seen systems that implemented DDD perfectly in small scale. When the systems got bigger, the exploding domain simply killed the project's ability to progress. The second part of the book is extremely useful for these instances.

However, DDD makes no reference to Dependency Injection (DI). At the time it was written DI was not as mature as it is today. DI is an enabler of many things, among them the bounded domain, distilled domain, abstract core and other highlighted insights of the DDD approach.

Clean Code & Code Complete

Clean Code and Code Complete are handbooks for developers looking to become experts in their profession. Clean Code refers to software development as art; Code Complete refers to coding as a Construction process.

Code Complete is older than Clean Code and has affected many in our profession. As it was revised in a second edition, you can see the influences of the Agile movement and of Martin Fawler's Refactoring book. Team leaders with whom I've spoken have defined either of the two as "lifechangers".

I do find Code Complete's discussion and advice on design issues very important. Their insistence on this conversation, especially in our times where Agile pushes everyone to start from bottom up, is an important reminder. Planning, system design, architecture, heuristic assumptions - they are all important when building big systems. Agile is a holistic approach which means it must be either used completely and perfectly- or it breaks. However, reality shows us that developers don't always do their job perfectly, and project constraints sometimes mean that there is no refactoring. Communication between people doesn't always work and code duplications sometimes show up in a large systems. Therefore, designing ahead is critically important. We all need to look back at what we've lost.

You won't find many who read both of these books because there is redundancy in the material. Code Complete, though, gives a bit more advice and is even more philosophical than Clean Code from time to time. Clean Code is indeed philosophical.

I would say that once you read Refactoring and Domain Driven Design and once you've refactored some systems and practiced software development by both building from scratch and maintaining existing systems, then reading these two books won't shake your world. Rather, you'll feel that you're getting closer to the top of your profession. The patterns are repeating and becoming clearer. The practice becomes more natural.

Resources

Management
http://en.wikipedia.org/wiki/Project_management_triangle
http://blogs.hbr.org/2014/01/if-youve-just-taken-over-a-team-quickly-let-underperformers-go/
http://venturebeat.com/2014/07/13/what-silicon-valley-refuses-to-learn-from-steve-jobs/
http://en.wikipedia.org/wiki/Project_management_triangle
"The Living Company":, Arie de Geus
Implementing Lean Software Development: From Concept to Cash, Poppendieck

Adler
Lecture notes by Ms. Ruth Dafni-Harel
http://www.gdnc.co.il/article.asp?Id=223
https://www.facebook.com/adlerins/posts/10150970368772992
http://onlinelibrary.wiley.com/doi/10.1002/jls.20003/citedby
http://jellycoach.blogspot.co.il/2013/05/blog-post_8.html
http://en.wikipedia.org/wiki/Affective_events_theory
http://cafe.themarker.com/topic/936561/
http://www.k6edu.com/4thgrade/social_studies/events-reactions-feelings.html
http://blog.ianuy.com/2010/09/26/on-the-high-turnover-rate-of-software-developers-or-how-to-retain-your-best-software-developers-and-programmers/
http://www.alfredadler.edu/about/theory
http://psychology.about.com/od/profilesal/p/alfred-adler.htm
http://www.studymode.com/essays/Action-Research-1785982.html
http://psychoanalyticbp.blogspot.co.il/2012/05/adlerian-theory.html
http://www.familyedcentre.org/who-we-are

Servant Leader
http://en.wikipedia.org/wiki/Servant_leadership#Characteristics
http://www.butler.edu/volunteer/resources/principles-of-servant-

leadership/

Scrum
http://en.wikipedia.org/wiki/Extreme_programming#Principles
http://en.wikipedia.org/wiki/Scrum_(software_development)#Sprint_planning_meeting
http://pm.stackexchange.com/questions/9909/should-a-scrum-master-also-perform-a-functional-manager-role
http://en.wikipedia.org/wiki/Agile_software_development
http://agilemanifesto.org/
http://www.infoq.com/resource/minibooks/Scrum_Primer/en/pdf/scrumprimer20.pdf
http://msdn.microsoft.com/en-us/library/ee191592(v=vs.100).aspx
http://pm.stackexchange.com/questions/3031/when-should-you-do-sprint-planning
https://www.scrumalliance.org/community/articles/2008/september/what-is-definition-of-done-(dod)
http://scrummethodology.com/
http://www.mountaingoatsoftware.com/agile/scrum/product-backlog
http://www.slideshare.net/tommynorman/project-management-with-scrum?next_slideshow=1
http://www.targetprocess.com/blog/tag/user-stories
http://www.scrumcrazy.com/User+Story+Life+Cycle+Diagram
http://ravikothiyal.blogspot.co.il/2014/07/scrum-sprint-calendar.html

Kanban
http://stefanroock.wordpress.com/2010/03/02/kanban-definition-of-lead-time-and-cycle-time/
http://leanandkanban.files.wordpress.com/2009/04/kanban-for-software-engineering-apr-242.pdf
http://www.targetprocess.com/blog/2009/05/lean-and-kanban-software-development.html
http://www.lean.org/FuseTalk/Forum/Attachments/Kanban%20for%20Software%20Development-Corbis.pdf

ScrumBan
https://www.youtube.com/watch?v=iLQWCbLjx50

118

Implementing Scrumban - www.SwitchingToScrum.com

Extreme Programming
https://7bsp1018.wikispaces.com/eXtreme+Programming

Books
http://www.infoq.com/minibooks/domain-driven-design-quickly